—A—
MOST
NOBLE
WATER

—A—
MOST
NOBLE
WATER

Revisiting
English Gin's Origins

Anistatia
MILLER
&
Jared
BROWN

Foreword by Alice Lascelles

MIXELLANY LIMITED

Cover design by: Tarek Salom
Text design by Anistatia R. Miller

First edition

British Library Cataloguing in Publication Data Available.

ISBN: 978-1-907434-59-4 (tradepaper);
ISBN: 978-1-907434-60-0 (hard cover)

THIS BOOK IS DEDICATED
TO OUR DEAR FRIENDS:
THE DISTILLERS, MIXERS,
AND SIPPERS OF GIN
AROUND THE WORLD!

WITH LOVE

contents

ALCHEMIST.

Impression of an alchemist from William Hone's 1832
The Year Book of Daily Recreation and Information
(Source: private collection).

Foreword

I MUST ADMIT, when I heard Anistatia and Jared had a new book about gin coming out my first thought was: dammit. For I knew it would almost certainly contain some kind of revelation that pulled the rug from under accepted drinks lore.

Because that's what Anistatia and Jared do, you see – they delight in upending the orthodoxy. Which makes them exciting but also, for a drinks writer like me, a little bit annoying – because it immediately renders everything I've written on the subject up to that point just a little bit flawed.

At least, in the case of *A Most Noble Water*, I can draw comfort from the fact that I'm not alone – because few stories in drinks have been as well- and as widely-rehearsed as the story of gin: that it's a direct descendent of Dutch genever, a juniper spirit English soldiers first got a taste for during Thirty Years War; and that it was popularised in England in the late 1600s by William of Orange; that the fall-out of this was the Gin Craze which blighted London's streets, swiftly followed by a nosedive in production...you know the drill.

Well, spoiler alert: according to this book, gin's ancestor was actually German. And that 'the knowledge of distilling spirits that included juniper berries had already reached English shores by 1527'. All the lurid tales accounts of the Gin Craze were simply 'tabloid puffery' (which will be a bit disappointing for any writer who's previously dined out on Hogarthian imagery).

For every bit of fake news the book quashes, though, it reveals something else possibly even more interesting. I was particularly intrigued to learn about the unsung role that women – both housewives and nobles – played in the evolution of distilling. And the popularisation of sipping spirits by the Elizabethans.

Aside from the historical facts, the book is also a treasure-trove of ancient recipes, some of which are quite dazzling in their complexity: a 16th century *aqua vitae* that calls for 50 ingredients including unicorn horn, myrrh, saffron, citrus and ambergris; and an aqua rosa solis, favoured by Elizabeth I, made with sundew flowers, spices and fruits, and tinted with gum amber, powdered pearl, coral and gold leaf. (Other recipes, rather less appetisingly, call for sulphuric acid, egg shells, turpentine and stills lined with lead – a reminder not to get too sentimental about how they did things back in the day.)

The book's authors are, of course, accomplished distillers in their own right; Jared is the co-founder and master distiller of Sipsmith, a company that paved the way for the contemporary craft gin movement. He brings this knowledge to bear re-creating one of the earliest gin recipes, which was then blind-tasted by some of today's leading practitioners of London Dry gin, in a nice bit of circularity.

The research is characteristically forensic: the pair dissect the eight gin acts (or statutes, as we learn) in meticulous detail, and hunt down information on female gin producers by scouring the archives of the Old Bailey.

But all this academic rigour is also imbued with a spirit of fun. This is a book about gin by two people who've made it their life —who make it, mix it, drink it, love it.

It made me think back to the first time I met Anistatia and Jared, about twenty years ago, at an international symposium organised by the Exposition Universelle des Vins et Spiritueux, a museum of vintage cocktail books, old spirits and wines on the pretty little island of Bendor in the south of France.

The pair had been charged with auditing the collection and putting the whole thing online (you can view the book catalogue for free at euvslibrary.com). And I was invited, along with the cream of the drinks world, to hear their findings for the first time.

Rather than delivering her lecture in a boardroom with Powerpoint, Anistatia (MA, MSc (Ox), soon-to-be PhD) did it standing knee-deep in the Mediterranean sea, while Jared waded around her, trousers rolled, mixing Martinis for the audience that had assembled on the beach. It was, like so much of what they do, nerdish in the extreme but also very punk.

These days my bookshelves are lined with their authoritative works on everything from vermouth and Cuban Cocktails to Harry Craddock and Martinis. Barely a week goes by when I don't consult the pages of something by Mixellany.

But as the pair are quick to remind us (cf Prof Barry Reay) 'There is no last word in the writing of history'; it's highly likely the story of gin will go through further iterations. Which is, as I say, frustrating, when your job involves committing things to print. But it's also, as I'm sure readers of this book will agree, what makes the study of it so fascinating.

—Alice Lascelles 29 May 2024

INTRODUCTION

W E OUGHT to begin with an apology: pretty much everything we thought we knew about gin history was wrong. For example, we recently discovered the origin story of gin was pure fiction, made up in 1804. After that, we lost count of the many other key points in gin history that were utterly inaccurate. In the process, we found the real story—and published the core in an academic journal to ensure it was carved in stone. No more myths and misconceptions. So, fasten your seatbelts, it's going to be a bumpy read. First a quick refresher about two of England's favourite alcoholic libations.

. Medieval historian Richard W. Unger reported that in '1574 more than half of London's beer breweries were owned and operated by aliens.'[1] He meant the Dutch. The link between hopped beer's Flemish (read: Dutch) origins and its fifteenth-century adoption in England is well-founded by both Unger and by medieval historian Peter Fleming, who concluded that while the city of Bristol supported a large transient migration of foreign sailors and merchants, its 'permanent, or semi-permanent population of "aliens" [the aforementioned Dutch]…was tiny', but they kickstarted the establishment of commercial beer breweries outside of London and Southampton.[2] However, there is no parallel evidence whatsoever that the Dutch imported their knowledge of distillation or their production of geneva, or that there was any Dutch influence on the English origins of juniper spirits at all. That trail quickly disappears under close examination, as you will see, while we take this journey from late medieval through Victorian England. We'll be looking at the recipes

---

1.   Richard W. Unger, *Beer in the Middle Ages and the Renaissance* (Philadelphia: University of Pennsylvania Press, 2004), 99.

2.   Peter Fleming, 'Time, Space and Power in Late Medieval Bristol' (unpublished working paper, University of West England, 2013), 104.

used, who made them, who sold them, and how the government tried to control them. (See, we didn't mention how drunk people got and how they did it.) Our attitude is that we leave the social history of gin to the social historians. (There are certainly a lot of specialists in English social history to tell that story.) Instead, we will present our findings about what was really produced that was or was not called gin plus who really invented it and produced it. We will also examine the stark historic differences in the production methods used to produce gins and genevas.

We also shine a light on the eight 'gin acts' (excise and regulatory acts aimed at British spirits production, sales, and regulation). There was no Gin Act of 1751. There was no London Gin Act. There were no acts titled 'gin act' that were devoted specifically to gin. We look at what each law actually did and, more importantly, did not do to gin production and sales rather than the usual examination of whether or not they had an effect on gin consumption. Finally, we will look into why there was a massive craze for gin drinking almost a century after the Gin Craze (1720-1751). (Okay, perhaps a little social history.)

Contrary to the conclusions found in the current piles of history books about the birth of English distillation, our research suggests that the arts of distillation and gin were not imported from the Low Countries—meaning Belgium, Holland, the Netherlands, and Luxembourg. Distillation techniques and the taste for juniper berries arrived in London from Germany long before the birth of geneva. We also pose a challenge that during the eighteenth century, there were two distinctly different English spirits being produced— one called geneva and the other simply called 'gin'. Current history treats these two spirits as parent and child rather than as fraternal twins from separate fathers.

We also suggest that despite what many historians have concluded, neither beer nor gin ever experienced a significant decline in production and sales in eighteenth-century England. We found that beer sales did not actually diminish even at the height of the Gin Craze. Instead, we propose another scenario unfolded as a combination of technological and stylistic advancements in brewing and distilling led to a revitalisation of English beer and spirits consumption during the nineteenth century. You see, ours is not a whiggish history fraught with platitudes about upward progress and enlightenment. It's simply a new way of looking at the story of the most significant spirit in the drinks world—and especially in the history of cocktails.

Why did we decide to delve so deep into gin's origins? The longstanding series of quandaries that surround gin's background struck a chord in 2008, when we were commissioned to research and write a history of the spirit for the Beefeater Gin distillery's visitor centre. Our curiosity continued while Anistatia earned two master's degrees in history and English local history, digging deep into the Bodelian Library at the University of Oxford, followed by four years spent developing her doctoral thesis, which looked at the evolution of English beer production, retailing, and regulation between the late fifteenth century and the early eighteenth century. She's really cut her teeth on excavating archives, now. Watch out. (In fact, this book is an extension of an article Anistatia published in 2023 in the academic journal *Brewing History* titled '"A most noble water of vertues": revisiting English gin's origins and its relationship with beer'.[3]) It's this latest research path has introduced us to an amazing cast of characters and given us an occasional opportunity to debate findings with a few key historians.

What you'll find in this book:

Gin didn't come from Holland or the Netherlands. We found four different stories about gin's birth, and we discovered none of them were true. English monks translated and learned about distillation from Arab alchemical texts in search of the 'water of life', rather than learning from the French or the Dutch. This information spread across England and Ireland and Scotland from that path.

---

3. Anistatia Miller, '"A most noble water of vertues": revisiting English gin's origins and its relatonship with beer', *Brewing History*, 195 (2023), 29-47.

German distillers and German house-wives were making juniper distillates before the Dutch. Then a German book of distillation formulas, written in 1500, was translated into English and sold in London in 1527. When the printing press gave birth to the publishing industry, books on distillation like this one spread across the UK, and collectively outsold the Bible. Meanwhile, the English royal court set a new trend, drinking spirits instead of just wines and beers. And the new middle class—who emulated the court's trends and styles—spread this drinking fashion which even trickled down to the poorer classes.

During the 1600s, we discovered that the start of a series of excise acts that regulated and taxed alcohol production didn't put an end to beer sales or boost gin sales. There were shifts in consumption, but these were social trends. Nothing more.

In the 1700s, there were no 'gin acts'. Heard of the 'gin acts'? They were actually eight statutes that regulated the production of all English spirits. One or two mentioned genever, but only as entry in a list of spirits. Gin was not mentioned in any of these acts. 'gin act' was a casual term applied to these acts around the time of their writing. And the Gin Craze? That was tabloid puffery, written to sell more newspapers. Yes, there were people selling gin on the streets, and people drank far more than today. But the reports of the time do not reflect the actual police records of the time. The whole thing got more and more exaggerated by later historians in subsequent centuries who took tabloid journalism as fact.

In the early nineteenth century, technological advances such as the invention of Sikes's hydrometer and the continuous column still caused a great leap forward in the quality of distilled spirits, which sparked a resurgence of consumer passion for spirits, and brought with it coffee houses, oyster bars and all manner of other new drinking establishments.

Which was the most impactful of the acts intended to control spirits production? The statute published on 27 June, 1825, did the following:

—set excise rates on hydrometer proof spirits;

—compelled distillers, rectifiers, spirits dealers, and spirits retailers to take out an annual £10 licence for each activity;

—prohibited any English distiller from owning a still with a capacity of less than 400 gallons;

—prohibited anyone who made beer, 'sweets' (we'll explain this later), vinegar, cider, perry, or refined sugar from distilling, rectifying, or compounding spirits on the same premises;

—and prohibited hawking, selling, or 'exposing to Sale' any spirits 'in or about the Streets, Highways or other Placed, or in or from any Boat or other Vessel upon the Water, or in any other Manner or Place whatsoever'.

Along the way, we found 39 recipes to back all of this up, from those first rudimentary distillates to the remarkable variety of formulae available to distillers in the mid-nineteenth century. (We also couldn't help add a few early modern drinks made with gin that kickstarted the relationship between gin and mixed drinks in general. (And in the Appendix, you'll find clues to the origins of Gin & Tonic.)

Finally, you're probably wondering about why we titled this book *A Most Noble Water*. That's simple. It was the name of a spirits recipe—'A Most Noble Water of Vertues'—found in the 1565 English translation of a Swiss distillation book titled *A New Booke of Destillatyon of Water, Called the Treasure of Euonymous*.[4] So make yourself your favourite cocktail or mixed drink made with London dry gin. (Dry martinis for us, thanks.) And get ready to take an adventurous ride through as close to the truth of the history of gin as we can manage—at this point in time. As New Zealand history professor Barry Reay commented in his 1996 book *Microhistories*: 'There is no last word in the writing of history.'[5] But we hope our findings will stand the test of time.

---

4.   Conrad Gessner and Peter Morwen, *A New Booke of Destillatyon of Waters, Called the Treasure of Euonymus* (London: John Day, 1565), 118.

5.   Barry Reay, *Microhistories: Demography, Society, and Culture in Rural England, 1800-1930* (Cambridge: Cambridge University Press, rev. ed. 2002), 262.

CHAPTER ONE

'...IDEAS GO ROUND AND ROUND'[6]

Gin didn't come from Holland. We found four
different stories about gin's birth, and we
discovered none of them were true.

THE LAST TIME we looked into gin's
birth, every book and article spoke of a
Dutch link between multi-grain genever
and rectified, single-grain gin. This narrative has
been bantered around among academics and the
general public—including ourselves—for decades.
But the facts are not as clear nor are the events
surrounding gin's origin story. We're not the only
ones to believe more research was needed to set

---

6. Stephen Bayley, *Gin* (Salisbury: Gin and Vodka Association
of Great Britain, 1994), 7.

the record on a straighter path. In his introduction to the Gin and Vodka Association's fiftieth-anniversary book in 1994, author Stephen Bayley remarked: 'Gin is one of those subjects that attracts myth. And like myth, stories about gin are repetitive. When you read the literature, you find that the ideas go round and round.'[7] It's true. We have a problem with the current history of gin, which echoes historian Jessica Warner's conclusion that 'in the mid-seventeenth century, the Dutch invented the beverage that is now known as gin'.[8] There are four storylines about this alleged origin of gin that parrot this Dutch connection.

The first fable tells us that gin came home with returning English troops who fought in the Low Countries in the late sixteenth century. According to historian John Burnett, gin was introduced in the aftermath of the 'experience of English soldiers in the Netherlands after

---

7. Stephen Bayley, *Gin* (Salisbury: Gin and Vodka Association of Great Britain, 1994), 7.

8. Jessica Warner, *Craze: Gin and Debauchery in an Age of Reason* (London: Profile Book, 2004), 24.

1570'.[9] Jessica Warner pointed to English physician Thomas Trotter's 1804 prohibitionist treatise, which tells us that:

> This vile habit, it appears, was less known in Britain three hundred years ago than it is at this time. Mr. Cambden [sic], in his Annals, under the year 1581, has made this remarkable observation:—The English, who hitherto had, of all the northern nations, shewn themselves least addicted to immoderate drinking, and been commended for their sobriety, first learned, in these wars in the Netherlands, to swallow large quantities of intoxicating liquors; and to destroy their own health by drinking that of others.[10]

---

9. John Burnett, *Liquid Pleasures: A Social History of Drink in Modern Britain* (London: Routledge, 1999), 161; John Watney, *Mother's Ruin: A History of Gin* (London: Peter Owen, 1976), 9-10.

10. Jessica Warner, 'The Naturalization of Beer and Gin in Early Modern England', *Contemporary Drug Problems*, 24/2 (1997), 386; Thomas Trotter, *An Essay, Medical, Philosophical, and Chemical on Drunkenness and its Effects on the Human Body* (London: Printed for T.N. Longman, and O. Rees, 1804), 140-141; William Camden, *THE HISTORIE OF THAT EVER Most blessed and Glorious Empresse, Queene ELIZABETH of happy renowne and matchlesse Fame* (London: Robert Vaughan, 1625), 5; R.W.W., 'Selections from Different Authors, &c.', *The Cottager's Monthly Visitor for M.DCC.XXI*, Vol. I (London: F.C. & J. Rivington, 1821), 333.

However, neither Trotter nor seventeenth-century historian William Camden (that's the correct spelling) directly referred to gin drinking as the target of these aspersions. And as Warner rightly noted, it is 'unclear whether contemporaries yet associated Dutch drinking habits with distilled spirits *per se*'—let alone with consuming gin, specifically.[11]

The second myth situates gin's nativity in Leyden, Netherlands. Burnett says, 'This spirit, redistilled over juniper berries, is credited to Professor Sylvius of Leyden University in the mid-sixteenth century.'[12] But an entry appearing in the 1815 edition of an encyclopaedia of American domestic economy suggests a seventeenth-century origin, telling us that:

> Among other things, juniper berries were tried by Sylvius, a professor of Leyden, who lived in the seventeenth century;... This liquor was

---

11.   Jessica Warner, 'The Naturalization of Beer and Gin in Early Modern England', *Contemporary Drug Problems*, 24/2 (1997), 386.

12.   John Burnett, *Liquid Pleasures: A Social History of Drink in Modern Britain* (London: Routledge, 1999), 161; John Watney, *Mother's Ruin: A History of Gin* (London: Peter Owen, 1976), 161.

accordingly first sold as a diuretic
in the apothecaries' shops; but as
it was drunk with avidity, it soon
became an article of trade...[13]

American medical writer for the *New Yorker* magazine Berton Roueché was not confident about the credibility of either claim when, in 1960, he hinted that: 'Exactly who was responsible for this procrastinated revelation is unclear, but the best evidence points to Franciscus Sylvius (or Franz de la Boë).'[14] Is there any evidence? Early modern historian Joop W. Koopmans, Associate Professor of Health Sciences Barclay W. Bakkum, and Professor André Parent tell us that Franciscus Sylvius (the Latinised name for Franciscus dele Boë) was a professor of both medicine and chemistry at the University of Leyden from 1658 until he

---

13.   Thomas Webster and Mrs. William, *An Encyclopædia of Domestic Economy* (New York: Harper & Brothers, 1815), 689.

14.   Berton Roueché, *The Neutral Spirit: A Portrait of Alcohol* (Boston: Little Brown and Company, 1960), 25.

died in 1672.[15] While Sylvius's interests in iatrochemistry (a sixteenth- and seventeenth-century approach to medicine and physiology applying principles found in chemistry) hints that he possibly experimented with distilling medicines, no surviving record confirms that he did indeed distil juniper berries with a grain spirit let alone that he originated a formula for such a liquid. So, Roueché's alleged evidence does not appear to exist. Furthermore, André Parent noted that Sylvius's 'scientific experiments but also his method of prescribing medication, which involved 'alkaloid- or acid-containing drugs' were harshly criticised by his contemporaries.[16] Parent's comment suggests neither academic nor commercial interest in Sylvius's experiments were forthcoming during the professor's lifetime. More recently, British

---

15.   Joop W. Koopmans, *Historical Dictionary of the Netherlands* (Lanham, MD: Rowman & Littlefield Publishers, 2015), 577-579; André Parent, 'Franciscus Sylvius on Clinical Teaching, Iatrochemistry and Brain Anatomy', *The Canadian Journal of Neurological Sciences*, 43 (2016), 596-603; Barclay Bakkum, 'A historical lesson from Franciscus Sylvius and Jacobus Sylvius', *Journal of Chiropractic Humanities*, 18(1) (2011), 94-98.

16.   André Parent, 'Franciscus Sylvius on Clinical Teaching, Iatrochemistry and Brain Anatomy', *The Canadian Journal of Neurological Sciences*, 43 (2016), 596-603.

journalist Ted Bruning discovered that the Dutch States General issued an ordinance in 1606—eight years before Sylvius's birth—that levied taxes on 'all distilled wine and anise, genever, and fennel waters' when sold as a beverage instead of as a medicine.[17] (This clearly indicates that genever was around 52 years before Professor Sylvius got his post at the university.)

The establishment of the Lucas Bols Distillery further confounds this story. Burnett claimed genever 'began to be manufactured on a commercial scale by Lucas Bols at Schiedam in 1575, and small quantities exported to England.'[18] However, there are three problems with his conclusion. First, the Bols Distillery did not change its name to the Lucas Bols Distillery until 1652, when Lucas took over the family business.[19] Sec-

---

17.   Ted Bruning, *London Dry: The Real History of Gin* (Hayward, CA: White Mule Press, 2020), 33.

18.   John Burnett, *Liquid Pleasures: A Social History of Drink in Modern Britain* (London: Routledge, 1999), 161; John Watney, *Mother's Ruin: A History of Gin* (London: Peter Owen, 1976), 161.

19.   The Lucas Bols Distillery, 'What a Distillery!', <http://www.lucasbols.com/history.asp> [accessed 12 February 2022]; 'Lucas Bols Distillery', <https:diffordsguide.com/> [accessed 12 February 2022].

ond, the only potential evidence that the company produced genever is a purchase receipt dated 1664 for juniper berries. And third, the knowledge of distilling spirits that included juniper berries had already reached English shores by 1527—a point we will soon discuss.

To further muddle matters, the third tale positions the accession of dual monarchs William of Orange and his wife Mary of England to the English throne in 1688 and their importation of genever as the launch point for the distillation and consumption of gin and other spirits in England.[20] This third story is frequently supported in the history books by referencing eighteenth-century journalist Daniel Defoe's assertion that 'strong waters' gained popularity after the first

---

20. Jessica Warner, 'The Naturalization of Beer and Gin in Early Modern England', *Contemporary Drug Problems*, 24/2 (1997), 387; Lucas Bols Distillery, '5 questions about Genever with Piet van Leijenhorst', <https://bols.com/bartendingacademy> [accessed 12 February 2022].

Anglo-Dutch war (1652-1654).[21] However, he did not directly attribute the monarchs with the introduction of genever to the royal court. Neither did he link them to the reason why spirits were popular in late seventeenth-century England. Instead, Defoe noted that 'In the Dutch War,...That the Captains of the Hollanders Men of War, when they were to engage with our Ships, usually set a Hogshead of Brandy abroach, afore the mast....'[22] By his account, Anglo-Dutch troops were exposed to brandy—not genever nor gin—before the monarchs' arrival. Yet the role their majesties played in shifting consumer preference takes an entirely different turn which we will also discuss later.

---

21.   Jessica Warner, 'The Naturalization of Beer and Gin in Early Modern England', *Contemporary Drug Problems*, 24/2 (1997), 388; Daniel Defoe, *A Brief Case of the Distillers, and of the Distilling Trade in England, shewing how far it is the interest of England to encourage the said trade, as it is so considerable an advantage to the landed interest, to the trade and navigation, to the publick revenue, and to the employment of the poor. Humbly recommended to the Lords and Commons of Great Britain, in the present Parliament assembled.* (London: Thomas Warner, 1725), 18.

22.   Daniel Defoe, *A Brief Case of the Distillers, and of the Distilling Trade in England, shewing how far it is the interest of England to encourage the said trade, as it is so considerable an advantage to the landed interest, to the trade and navigation, to the publick revenue, and to the employment of the poor. Humbly recommended to the Lords and Commons of Great Britain, in the present Parliament assembled.* (London: Thomas Warner, 1725), 18.

The fourth and most common myth of gin's birth stories cites English soldiers' return from the Thirty Years War (1618-1648). It was said that they fought alongside Dutch soldiers and were impressed with their prowess in battle, with credit given to their flasks of 'Dutch Courage'. They returned to England with a thirst for this Dutch spirit and demand was met with a supply both from imported spirits and domestic production fostered—even in this version of gin's birth—by England's only Dutch King, William III of Orange. There is scant evidence that Dutch soldiers were drinking genever at all. In fact, when William of Orange visited his palace at Het-Loo, his physician Walter Harris was so impressed he wrote a book in 1699 about its gardens (which have been compared to those of Versailles). As an addendum, he wrote *A Short Account of Holland,* describing life there, devoting pages and pages to accounts of food and drink. There was no mention of genever, but he talked at length about the local love of wine infused with wormwood—vermouth. On this he wrote the following:

They have also every where their Wormwood wine which is commonly called by the Name of Alsom Wine and by the English for sound sake Wholesome Wine and the which they do not drink only for a Whet before Dinner or on Physical accounts but indifferently at any time of the Day or Evening. It is made of the French Wine before mentioned and by its Bitterness does take off that lusciousness or nauseous taste to Strangers.[23]

This Dutch-English link to gin even found its way into the Oxford English Dictionary, which declared: 'Gin was originally made by Dutch distillers in the late sixteenth cent[ury].'[24] However, the definition added an intriguing point that: 'In the mid 18th cent. a less coarse, more subtly flavoured gin began to be produced in London (hence known as London gin).' Despite these authoritative declarations, a question is raised: When

---

23.   Walter Harris, *A description of the king's royal palace and gardens at Loo, together with a short account of Holland* (London: R. Roberts, 1699), 35.

24.   Oxford English Dictionary, 'gin, n.1a'.

Frontipiece from John Shirley's 1687 book The accomplished ladies rich closet of rarities: or, The ingenious gentlewoman and servant-maids delightfull companion: Containing many excellent things for the accomplishment of the female sex, after the exactest manner and method, viz. *(Source: private collection).*

and how did the English learn to distil spirits and especially when did they first learn to make a 'coarse' version of gin that later became a 'more subtly flavoured gin' that was specifically produced in London? For those of you who have read our books before—particularly *Spirituous Journey: A History of Drink, Volume One*—you know we cannot resist winding the clock back a few centuries and camping ourselves in the Moorish-occupied Iberian Peninsula (read: Spain, Portugal, and part of southern France).[25] That's where our travels begin.

25.   Anistatia R. Miller and Jared M. Brown, *Spirituous Journey: A History of Drink, Volume One* (London: Mixellany Limited, 2009), passim.

CHAPTER TWO

'IT comes LIKe ` rosewater'[26]

German distillers and housewives made
juniper distillates before the Dutch. Then a
German distillation book written in 1500, was
translated into English and sold in London in
1527.

I N THE SAME WAY distilling in Italy and
France was born, England also owes a debt
of gratitude to eighth- and ninth-century Arab alchemists. The seeds of distillation
sprouted in England when several English academics journeyed to the Near East and Spain dur-

---

26.   Ya'qub ibn Ishaq Al-Kindi, *Kitab al-Taraffuq fial-`itr*, MS Top-
kapi Sarai, Istanbul, No. 62-1992, folios 140-141; Karl Garbers, *Kitab
kimiya' al-'itr wat-tas idat : Buch über die Chemie des Parfüms und
die Destillationen; ein Beitrag zur Geschichte der arabischen Parfümchemie und Drogenkunde aus dem 9* (Leipzig: Brockhaus, 1948), 95.

ing the twelfth century, returning with a wealth of scientific knowledge that was ripe for translation. Latin was the preferred language for sharing information amongst monastic and scholarly compatriots. It was a reasonably universal and an effective way to conceal knowledge from the prying eyes of the public.[27] (Although it wasn't great for hiding ideas from members of the Church's courts of the Inquisition!) Quickly, certain texts related to English scholars come to mind: Adelard of Bath's translation of Arabic mathematical treatises into Latin; Robert of Ketton's translation of Arabic astrological tracts into Latin; and most notably Robert of Chester's translation into Latin and compilation of the works of the ninth-century Iraqi alchemist al-Kindi, Persian alchemist and physician al-Razi, and Irani alchemist Jabir ibn Hayyan or Geber.

Published in 1144, Robert of Chester's *Liber de Compositione Alchimae* [Book on the Com-

---

27.   Aisha Alowais and Mesut Idriz, 'Adelard of Bath', Al-Adab Journal, 1/139 (2021), 33; G.J. Toomer, 'The Medieval Background', *Eastern Wisdom and Learning: The Study of Arabic in Seventeenth-century England* (Oxford: Oxford University Press, 1996), 7-13.

position of Alchemy] is generally considered to be the first work to appear in England that included distillation theories and techniques.[28] With this translation and other works that came after it, English academics and aspiring alchemists learned that al-Kindi searched for a digestible *al'iksir* [elixir] that was intended to promote overall well-being and to potentially prolong life. The book detailed how to extract the essence of wine by employing an *al-anbîq* [alembic]—a basic distillation device—with the conclusion that: 'so wine is distilled in wetness and it comes like rosewater in colour.'[29] Inspired by this revelation, English physician Gilbertus Anglicus's encyclopedic work *Compendium Medicinæ* [Compendium of Medicines] which was written around 1230 to 1250, made frequent mention of *aqua vitæ* and *aqua*

28.   Robert Halleux, 'The Reception of Arabic Alchemy in the West', *Encyclopedia of the History of Arabic Science. Vol. 3*, ed. by Roshdi Rashed (London: Routledge, 1996), 889-890.

29.   Ya'qub ibn Ishaq Al-Kindi, *Kitab al-Taraffuq fial-`itr*, MS Topkapi Sarai, Istanbul, No. 62-1992, folios 140-141; Karl Garbers, *Kitab kimiya' al-'itr wat-tas idat : Buch über die Chemie des Parfüms und die Destillationen; ein Beitrag zur Geschichte der arabischen Parfümchemie und Drogenkunde aus dem 9* (Leipzig: Brockhaus,, 1948), 95.

ardens as medicinal preparations.[30] Books like Chester's and Anglicus's were read in the first bastions of English scientific knowledge—the libraries housed in monasteries.

The arrival of Franciscan friars on English shores in 1224, heralded the foundation of monastic libraries in London, Oxford, Cambridge, York, Salisbury, Hereford, Worcester, and Newcastle. This is seen in a 'Union Catalogue' that systematically recorded the collection of works authored by over 80 ancient and medieval scholars.[31] The catalogue included tracts by the Uzbekistani alchemist Avicenna, who once remarked that 'the body acts as a distilling apparatus' in which the stomach serves as a cucurbit—or still pot—and the head collects the humours in the same manner as an *al-anbîq*'s conical head allows vapours to rise.[32]

---

30. Linda Ehrsam Voigts, 'The Master of the King's Stillatories', in *The Lancastrian Court, Harlaxton Medieval Studies 13* (Donington: Shaun Tyas, 2003) 233-252.

31. W.R. Jones, 'Franciscan Education and Monastic Libraries: Some Documents', *Traditio*, 30 (1974), 435-434.

32. R. J. Forbes, *Short History of the Art of Distillation: From the Beginnings up to the Death of Cellier Blumenthal* (Leiden: Brill, 1948), 39.

Access to this treasure trove of knowledge intensified the curiosity of the Somerset-born, Oxford-educated Franciscan friar Roger Bacon.[33] Lecturing at Oxford until 1237, Bacon took a post at the University of Paris. While he was there, one of his colleagues was the German Dominican friar Albertus Magnus, who also expressed his interest in distillation. Magnus's appraisal of the distilling process concluded that: 'the alchemist requires two or three rooms exclusively devoted to sublimations, solutions, and distillations.'[34] (Never mind the fact that Bacon thought Magnus was dubiously treated like an academic rock star when he arrived in Paris and was not about to

33.   Robert Adamson, 'Roger Bacon', *Encyclopaedia Britannica*, Ninth Edition, Vol 3 (Chicago: Encyclopaedia Britannica, 1911), 153-154; Norbert Kockmann, '200 Years in Innovation in Distillation', *ChemBioEng Reviews* 1/1 (2014), 41; Steven J. Williams, 'Roger Bacon and the *Secret of Secrets*' in *Roger Bacon and the Sciences: Commemorative Essays*, ed. Jeremiah Hackett (New York: Brill, 1997), 366.

34.   Norbert Kockmann, '200 Years in Innovation in Distillation', *ChemBioEng Reviews* 1/1 (2014), 41.

join the German's growing fan club.[35]) But enough about Magnus for the moment.

Bacon entered the Franciscan order in 1256 and continued his research in France while awaiting funding for his return home. After he re-established himself back at Oxford, he published his *Opus Majus* [Major Work] in 1267, presenting his observations of mathematics, optics, astronomy, and, of course, alchemy.[36] He recounted in his notes that he purchased 'secret books' for about twenty years, possibly including 'compilations of recipes, formulas. and "experiments"'.[37] There are no surviving records to confirm the contents of Bacon's collection. But historian Bruce T Moran surmised that through his research of these works, Bacon sought 'a super-medicine, an elixir or *aqua*

35.   Richard LeMay, 'Roger Bacon's Attitude toward the Latin Translations and Translators of the Twelfth and Thirteenth Centuries,' *Roger Bacon and the Sciences: Commemorative Essays*, ed. Jeremiah Hackett (New York: Brill, 1997), 25-47.

36.   Robert Adamson, 'Roger Bacon', *Encyclopaedia Britannica*, Ninth Edition, Vol 3 (Chicago: Encyclopaedia Britannica, 1911), 153-154.

37.   Steven J. Williams, 'Roger Bacon and the *Secret of Secrets*' in *Roger Bacon and the Sciences: Commemorative Essays*, ed. Jeremiah Hackett (New York: Brill, 1997), 366.

vitae that could purify physical bodies of their impurities, rid the human body of disease, and prolong life.'[38] To achieve this aim, Bacon strove to 'reduce substances to their simple essence.'[39] In other words, he spent a lot of time distilling things. While infusion was the most common extraction method for making medicines at the time, it yielded a less potent, tea-like result. Bacon agreed with Avicenna's theory that fermenting medicines improved their potency. By distilling those ferments, he concluded that all 'healing oils [or essences] ought to be prepared by alchemical

---

38.   Bruce T Moran, *Distilling Knowledge: Alchemy, Chemistry, and the Scientific Revolution* (London: Harvard University Press, 2005), 11.

39.   Faye Getz, 'Roger Bacon and Medicine: the paradox of the Forbidden Fruit and the Secrets of Long Life,' in *Roger Bacon and the Sciences: Commemorative Essays*, ed. by Jeremiah Hackett (New York: Brill, 1997), 350-351.

Next pages from an anonymous fifteenth-centurry manuscript, detailing how to make Elixir Aqua Vite and Roger Bacon's Elixir Vite (Source: Bodleian Library).

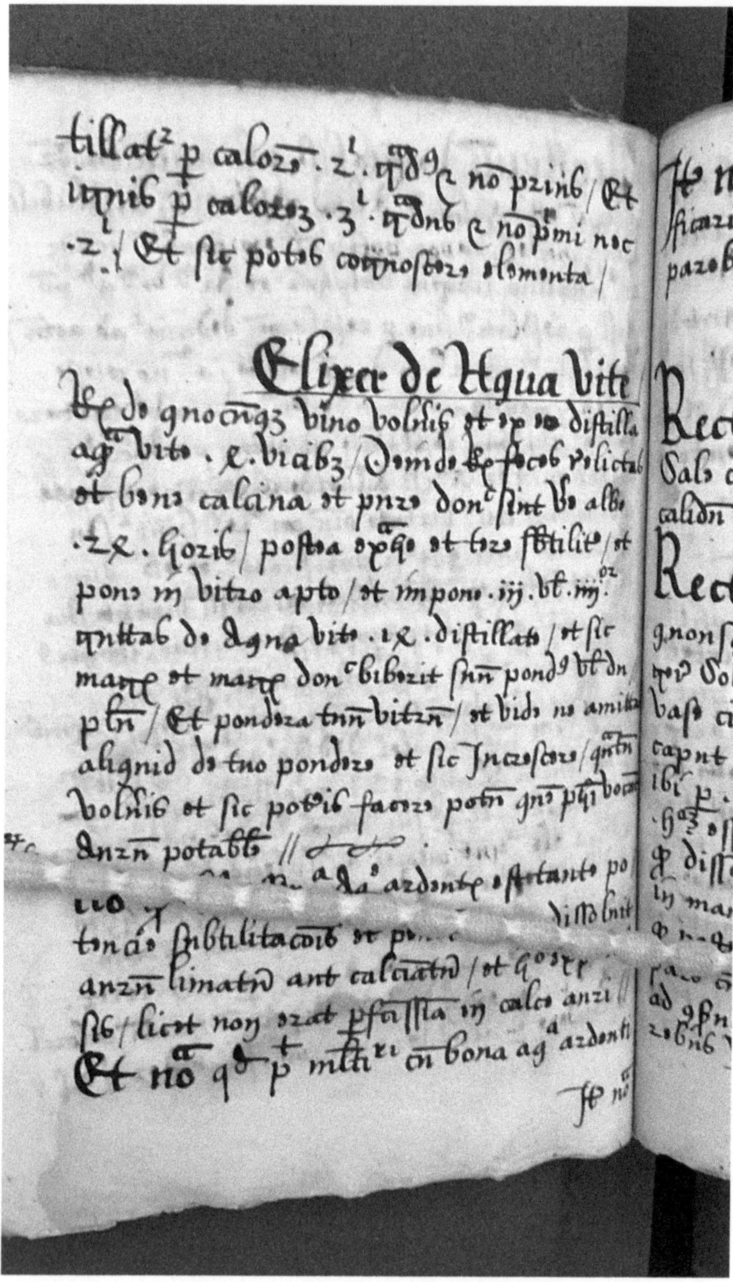
Elixer de Aqua vite

...gn̄s cōgz̄ ſpm bib bn̄ ſublimatꝯ ꝟt ſcib
ꝯt ab ipo · Λ · viab9 diſtilla lnnaziaz gn̄a
ſaib ꝯt fixabit² ꝯt ꝯzit tn̄z̄ ſſibilis //
.... mortꝯ ..
...ꝯꝰ bini ꝯt flenmatꝯ ſopatn̄ p · t · ꝯ ·
ꝰiꝯb rovatn̄ ſpicꝯ ꝗtinnꝰ ī balnꝰo fimi vali //
diſſi¹ dꝯpnzarꝯ ꝗ ꝗito ꝯſt ꝯꝑn9 gꝺ ꝯtꝯlliꝯꝛim9
diꝰ ꝗ tꝯ minimꝰ alloꝯnti ſnm9 ꝑ ꝗuo ꝗꝺ mtꝯl //
ꝯirꝑnt mꝯꝯ ꝯſp bnlꝗi //
Calor fimi ꝯſt caloz in p̄mo ꝯꝗ dn̄ .
Caloz balnꝰi ꝯſt caloz m̄ · z̄° · ꝗzadn̄ .
Caloz ꝯiꝯis ꝯſt caloz ī · z̄ · ꝗzadn̄ .
Caloz arꝯns ꝟt fflams ī · ꝯ° · ꝯꝗ dn̄ .

Elixer vite ſꝙ m̄ magiꝝm Rogerm̄
Bacon in libzo ꝯpiſtali oīa Jncōmoda
ꝯonſoꝯtnꝯrꝰmoboꝰns ꝯt bitꝰ cordis ꝯ corpis
ſoꝛnans, ꝯf ambre · z̄ · β · margaritaꝛ · z̄ · ij ·
floris roſemarini · z̄ · iij · ligni aloes · z̄ · j ·
ꝯarnis ſoꝛpentꝯ pond9 · j · ꝯꝺ Auri potabilis ·
· z̄ · iiij · oſſis de cordꝯ ꝯꝛni · z̄ · j · ꝗ° aſſꝑn° ſan //
ꝛtnis ꝗuani · z̄ · m̄ · ꝯ bn̄ miſtꝯant² · //

Laus deo in ebū,

means through distillation.'[40] (Evidence of Bacon's work lived on in fifteenth- and sixteenth-century English manuscripts that roughly described how to make *Elixir Vite* and *Elixir Aqua Vite*.[41])

Perhaps it was Bacon's fame. Perhaps it was his 1267 book that were responsible for igniting interest in distillation in the British Isles. Or maybe it was the work of Peter of Ireland (aka: Petrus de Ibernia), who studied and taught at Oxford, Paris, and Toledo, who was equally intrigued by the works of Arab alchemist Avicenna.[42] Either way, word spread to Ireland. In *Liber Ruber* [Red Book]— a series of pre-1360s documents compiled by Bishop Richard Ledrede of Ossory, Ireland—two folios are of interest. Folio 62 is a treatise on the making of *aqua vitæ*, which

---

40.   Faye Getz, 'Roger Bacon and Medicine: the paradox of the Forbidden Fruit and the Secrets of Long Life,' in *Roger Bacon and the Sciences: Commemorative Essays*, ed. by Jeremiah Hackett (New York: Brill, 1997), 350-351.

41.   Bodleian Library, MS Ashmole 1441.

42.   M.B. Crow, 'Peter of Ireland: Teacher of St Thomas Aquinas', *Studies: An Irish Quarterly Review*, 45/180 (1956), 443-456.

was translated into English and published in the *Ulster Journal of Archaeology* in 1858:[43]

> Aqua vitæ is either simple or compound. The simple is that which, without any mixture, is drawn from wine, and is called aqua vini; and this, being drawn simply, should in like manner be used simply, without any mixture with wine or water. Simple aqua vitæ is to be made in the following manner: take choice one-year-old wine, and rather of a red than a thick sort, strong and not sweet, and place it in a pot, closing the mouth with a clepsydra [water clock] made of wood, and having a linen cloth rolled around it; out of which the pot there is to issue a lyne arm (cavalis) leading to another vessel having a worm. This latter vessel is to be kept filled with cold water, frequently renewed when it grows warm and the water foams through the cavalis. The pot with the wine having been placed previously on the fire, distil it with a slow fire until you

---

43.   RCB Library: D11/12, *Red Book of Ossory*, folio 62.

have from it one-half of the quantity
of wine that you put in.[44]

There seems to be some confusion about the translator's use of the word 'clepsydra', since the term refers to a 'water clock'. But, the 'lyne arm' or 'cavalis' can be interpreted as the line arm that joins the column and the neck to the condenser system, which greatly impacts the reflux during the distillation process. Furthermore, the meaning of the term *'aqua vitæ'* changes a few times over the centuries, which we explain later. Here, the author used a word to describe a single distillate extracted from wine. Folio 64 contains a 'Tract on different kinds of waters' which summarises twelve different 'waters', the first titled *'De aqua rubicunda'* [Of the Red Water], which was a recipe for making a red wine distillate. [45] According to historian Pearl Kibre, this recipe

---

44. G.B. (n.d.), 'On the Early Use of Aqua Vitæ in Ireland', *Ulster Journal of Archaeology*, volume 6 (1858), 283-293.

45. RCB Library: D11/12, *Red Book of Ossory*, folio 64; Hugh Jackson Lawlor, 'Calendar of the Liber Ruber of the Diocese of Ossory', *Proceedings of the Royal Irish Academy: Archaeology, Culture, History, Literature*, 27 (1908), 187; Pearl Kibre, 'Alchemical Writings Ascribed to Albertus Magnus,' *Speculum*, 17/4 (Oct 1942), 504-505.

was ascribed to Roger Bacon's colleague at the University of Paris—the German alchemist Albertus Magnus.[46] The next stop takes us to Scotland. Evidence shows us that by the late fifteenth century, Bénédictine monks in Scotland distilled spirits as well. An entry in the 1494 Scottish Exchequer Roll noted that: 'The delivery was made by Brother John Cor, by order of accounts controller, he says, by order of the king to make aquavitæ within this account, 8 boles of malt.'[47] This document illustrates that James IV of Scotland requested Bénédictine monk John Cor—who was in the king's service—to produce a malted-barley distillate called *aqua vitæ* for his Majesty's consumption.[48] Today, we call this Scottish spirit 'new make' whisky. But there is a catch in using

46. Pearl Kibre, 'Alchemical Writings Ascribed to Albertus Magnus,' *Speculum*, 17/4 (Oct 1942), 504-505.

47. Scotland, 'Exchequer Roll (Edinburgh, 1494), Accounts of Ballivi ad Extra, Stirling, 18 June 1494 to 12 August 1495,' in *Accounts of the Lord High Treasurer of Scotland, vol. 1* (Edinburgh 1877), ccxiv, 100, and 232. A bole or boll has been occasionally cited as a dry measure weighing approximately 320 lbs.

48. While current marketing materials distributed by the Lindores Abbey suggest Corr was a Bénédictine monk of the Order of Tiron, which relocated in 1190 from France to the Lindores Abbey in Scotland, no primary source has been located to date that substantiates this claim.

this piece of evidence. Historian Constance Anne Wilson reminded us here that 'Scottish alcoholic spirits were always named as *aqua vitæ* in documents until the eighteenth century and beyond' and thus were not related to the *aqua vitæ* produced by the English and Irish, which did include botanicals.[49] (We promise we'll talk about this later.) So, let's take the next leap in time to talk about how we progressed from making what we call today 'new-make' to making spirits flavoured with botanicals.

'waTer oF Geniper Berries'[50]

LET'S HEAD TO GERMANY, where fifteenth- and sixteenth-century housewives not only brewed beer, they distilled it with juniper berries, making a cheaper version of the profitable juniper berry brandy that their male counterparts produced commer-

---

49. Constance Anne Wilson, *Water of Life: A History of Wine-Distilling and Spirits 500 BC to AD 2000* (Totnes, Devon: Prospect Books, 2006), 150.

50. Laurens Andrewe, *The vertuose boke of distyllacyon of the water of all maner of herbes* (London: Laurens Andrewe, 1527), 258-259.

cially in cities such as Augsburg, near Munich.[51] By the mid-sixteenth century, the city's male brandy distillers and brandy sellers were already organised into a Brandymaker's Craft (*Branndt-weinbrenner Handwerk*).[52] Yes, we know, the most notable reports of medieval European distillation centre around the work of twelfth-century Italian physicians Salernus and Barthelomaeus of Salerno. However, the links between early English and European distillation point to this German origin. It's not so far-fetched. Don't forget the rock-star alchemist Albertus Magnus hailed from Germany.[53] He obviously helped spread the word about distillation on his home turf. Historians B. Anne Tlusty and R. J. Forbes tell us that in Germany, spirits distillation 'began as a home

---

51.   B. Ann Tlusty, 'Water of Life, Water of Death: The Controversy over Brandy and Gin in Early Modern Augsburg,' *Central European History*, 31/1 (1998), 14.

52.   B. Ann Tlusty, 'Water of Life, Water of Death: The Controversy over Brandy and Gin in Early Modern Augsburg,' *Central European History*, 31/1 (1998), 14.

53.   R. J. Forbes, *Short History of the Art of Distillation: From the Beginnings up to the Death of Cellier Blumenthal* (Leiden: Brill, 1948), 57-58.

industry, unlike in France and Italy, where it seems to have been practised primarily in monasteries.'[54]

Tlusty qualified her claim, explaining that the distilling of grain spirits was 'originally associated with alchemists and then with the "old women" (*alte Weiber*) or "waterburners" (*Wasserbrennerinnen*)' who employed the technique as 'part of their herbal cures' because 'economically disadvantaged craftsmen, and poorer craftsmen's wives…could not afford to distil wine or buy and sell taxed brandy.'[55] Naturally, folks who produced grain spirits did not have the protections of a guild or citizenship to protect them from falling afoul of the law. For example, in Augsburg, Caspar Lorer and his wife were caught distilling grain spirits.[56] (At least she was, but he was culpable.) He

---

54. B. Ann Tlusty, 'Water of Life, Water of Death: The Controversy over Brandy and Gin in Early Modern Augsburg,' *Central European History*, 31/1 (1998), 8; R. J. Forbes, *Short History of the Art of Distillation: From the Beginnings up to the Death of Cellier Blumenthal* (Leiden: Brill, 1948), 102.

55. B. Ann Tlusty, 'Water of Life, Water of Death: The Controversy over Brandy and Gin in Early Modern Augsburg,' *Central European History*, 31/1 (1998), 8.

56. B. Ann Tlusty, 'Water of Life, Water of Death: The Controversy over Brandy and Gin in Early Modern Augsburg,' *Central European History*, 31/1 (1998), 22.

claimed he had no knowlegde of her actions and she admitted that she needed a source of income that allowed her to stay at home with their six childen. Caspar was held responsible and was fined over 200 gulden—an amount equal to 'several years' income for a poorer craftsman'.[57] In lieu of payment, Caspar was banished from the city, then was pardoned two months later and permitted to return home.[58] But then Tlusty reminded us that the Lorers and especially Mrs Lorer were not the only ones to be caught making grain spirits. So, how did the techniques for distilling spirits break the barricade of secrecy held in close guard by guilds and spread throughout Germany? And then how did that information make its way to England?

It all started when German craftsman Johannes Gutenberg invented the printing press during the 1430s. His creation led to an information revolution, which contributed to the wide

57.   B. Ann Tlusty, 'Water of Life, Water of Death: The Controversy over Brandy and Gin in Early Modern Augsburg,' *Central European History*, 31/1 (1998), 22.

58.   B. Ann Tlusty, 'Water of Life, Water of Death: The Controversy over Brandy and Gin in Early Modern Augsburg,' *Central European History*, 31/1 (1998), 22.

dispersal of knowledge about distillation.[59] An historian best known for her work on the profound effect of printing on Western civilisation, Elizabeth L. Eisenstein noted that 'practical guidebooks and manuals also became more abundant, making it easier to lay plans for getting ahead in the world.'[60] Learning new techniques such as distillation offered housewives and alchemists fresh ways to preserve essential ingredients for making medicines. Two printed books leapt off the shelves and got Germany and Austria into the distilling trade.

Viennese physician Michael Puff von Schrick's 24-page treatise *Von allen geprenten wassern* [From all waters printed] documented 82 herbal distillates, including *kramat-peer* or *wachalter-peer wasser* (also called *wacholderbeer-wasser* [juniper berry water])—a juniper-berry distillate that Puff von Schrick credited to (drum

---

59. Hellmut E. Lehmann-Haupt, 'Johannes Gutenberg'. *Encyclopedia Britannica*, 18 May. 2023 <https://www.britannica.com/biography/Johannes-Gutenberg> [accessed 16 August 2023].

60. Elizabeth L. Eisenstein, *The Printing Revolution in Early Modern Europe* (Cambridge: Cambridge University Press, 1983), 53.

Cover of Michael Puff von Schrick's Von Allen Geprenten
(Source: private collection).

Ein nutzlich puch-
lein von allen gebrantē wassern
Gerechtfertiget auß dem newen
distillir buch.

Cover of Michael Puff von Schrick's Von den ausgerbranntan
wassern *(Source: private collection).*

¶ Von Kramat peer oder Wachalter peer.
¶ Wie ist zumercken die tugent der Krammat peer nach laut und sage
meyster Alberti des beyden/die man hat bewæret vnd verfuche zu Flo-
rentz in der stat.
¶ Item zu dem ersten/so nym die Kramat peer zu der zeyt vnser lieben
frawen verschiebung wie vill du wilt/vnnd seid die in einem newen
hafen/geuß daran den besten weyn so du jm gehaben magst/setz das
zu dem feür vnd laß es wol erwallen/seym es reyn vnd sawber/wenn
das geschehen ist/so geuß den weyn ab den peeren in ein reynes glaß/
vnd behalt das schon bedeckt.
¶ Darnach nym desselben weyns auß dem vaß/da der erst weyn auß
gelassen worden ist/vñ geuß den selbigen wein auff die gesotten Krammat peer/thu jm recht als vor der erst wein gesotten ist/vnd geuß jm
ab als du dem ersten gethan hast.
¶ Darnach nym die köuner vnd leg sie auff ein pieet/trucken sie wol ab
an dem lufft/wenn sie dann trucken werden/so thu sie in ein vaß oder
in ein krug/vñ geuß daran sißen morgen oder neun also bescheydenlich
alle tan ve ein wenin.

A page decribing a juniper spirit in Michael Puff von Schrick's
Von Allen Geprenten *(Source: private collection).*

roll please) German alchemist Albertus Magnus.[61]

Printed in 1476, Puff von Schrick's volume was
the first mass-produced book to contribute to the
spread of spirits consumption beyond its use as a
'panacea for a multitude of medical complaints'.[62]
By 1500, it was reprinted 38 times. His earlier

61. Michael Puff von Shrick, *Von allen geprenten wassern*, (Augsburg: n.p. 1481); Heironymous Brunschiwg, *Libre de arte distillandi*
(Strasbourg: Johann Grüninger, 1500), folio 20.

62. B. Ann Tlusty, 'Water of Life, Water of Death: The Controversy
over Brandy and Gin in Early Modern Augsburg,' *Central European
History*, 31/1 (1998), 9.

work, the 14-page *Von den ausgerbranntan wassern* [From Burned Waters] also outlined the pharmaceutical use of distilled herbs. (Written in 1455 and revised in 1466, the book did not 'treat the method of distilling, but exclusively of the medical uses of the extracts distilled from about 70 flowers and herbs' and was printed posthumously in 1500.[63])

It was the best-selling *Von allen geprenten wassern* and the lucrative profits reaped by the growing number of German commercial brandy distillers who made *wachalter-peer wasser*—a juniper spirit made with wine distillate—that elevated German drinking culture to a new level. It also triggered the manufacture of *cramatbeerwasser*— a spirit distilled from beer and juniper berries, which as we said before was produced by 'poor widows, economically disadvantaged craftsmen, and poorer craftsmen's wives, who could not afford to distil wine', according to Tlusty.[64] This spirit

---

63.   Wellcome Collection, explanation in *Von den ausgerbranntan wassern* <https://wellcomecollection.org/works/pakjtgzm/images> [accessed 16 November 2023].

64.   B. Ann Tlusty, 'Water of Life, Water of Death: The Controversy over Brandy and Gin in Early Modern Augsburg,' *Central European History*, 31/1 (1998), 21.

offered the poor a chance to have fun, too. This *cramatbeerwasser* is one of the first documented associations of beer being used as a fermented grain base for the distillation of a neutral spirit. From this inception, the link between English and German distillation was solidified with the publication of the second German distillation book.

German surgeon and botanist Hieronymous Brunschwig's book *Libre de arte distillandi* [Learn about the art of distilling]—also printed in 1500—was more widely distributed outside of Germany than Puff von Schrick's more than three dozen editions of *Von allen geprenten wassern*. Brunschwig's volume was translated and published first in Brussels in 1517, then in London by Laurens Andrewe on 18 April 1527 under the title *The vertuose boke of distyllacyon of the waters of all maner of herbes*, and finally in Czechoslovakia in 1559.[65]

Along with a review of various types and styles of stillatories used to extract essences and

---

65.   Volker Fritz Brüning, *Bibliographica Alchemica* (Munich: K G Saur Verlag GmbH, 2004), 18-19.

Cover of Hieronymous Burnschwig's Libre de arte distillandi
(Source: private collection).

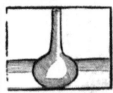

Pages from Brunschwig's book depicting different styles of stills (above) and a recpe for Water of Juniper (below) (Source: private collection).

distillation techniques, the book highlighted the benefits of numerous herbal distillates, including one for a 'Water of Geniper berries' which was recommended for the treatment of 'the gravell in the lymmes and in the bladder.'[66] Bottom line is that Puff von Schrick's and Brunschwig's works predated the Low Countries treatise most frequently mentioned in English gin's historiography—*Een constelijck distileerboec* [A constellation distillery]. Written in 1552 by Belgian surgeon Philippis Hermanni, this book featured a *Geneverbessen* [Juniper berries] distillate. [67] However, Hermanni's work was not translated into English. Therefore, it would not have been as easily accessed or adopted by England's budding group of distilling housewives and alchemists.

Okay, so the Dutch-English links to spirits distilled with juniper berries still frequently appear in the history books. A claim made by Genever Museum Director Eric van Schoonen-

66.   Laurens Andrewe, *The vertuose boke of distyllacyon of the water of all maner of herbes* (London: Laurens Andrewe, 1527), 258-259.

67.   Philippus Hermanni, *Een Constelijck Distileerboec* (Antwerp: Philip de Lens, 1552), 56.

berghe, in 1996, suggested that an unpublished formula written in Middle Dutch predated Hermanni's 1552 recipe.[68] The tract titled *Gebrande wyn te maken* [How to make brandy] was promoted by modern-day gin producer Maison Villevert as a missing link in the story of gin, claiming it was written in 1495.[69] The recipe von Schoonenberghe identified was included in what he called a 'compilation of medical and scientific formulas' acquired by Sir Hans Sloane, who bequeathed the manuscripts upon his death, in 1753, to the newly founded British Museum.[70] However, the British Library's online catalogue entry for the Sloane MS345 compendium initiated an immediate misinterpretation. The entry dated the compilation to circa 1500 and stated the formula in question was part of a:

---

68.   Eric van Schoonenberghe, *Jenever in de Lage Landen* (Brugge: Stuchting Kunstboek, 1996), 49-50.

69.   Gin Guild, 'The 1495 Gin', <https://www.thginguild.com/ginopedia/> [accessed 18 December 2020]; Eric van Schoonenberghe, *Jenever*, 49-50; Various, *Medische En Technische Middelnederlandse Recepten*, ed. Willy L. Braekman (Ghent: Koninklijke Vlaamse Academie, 1975), 211-212.

70.   Eric van Schoonenberghe, *Jenever in de Lage Landen* (Brugge: Stuchting Kunstboek, 1996), 49-50.

Sloane MS 345

Date	c. 1500
Title	A compendium of medical and scientific texts with a calendar
Content	Contents: ff. 1r-6r: Reyner Oesterhusen, Doctor of Deventer, Holland, Compendium medicinale, with a prologue addressed to the Bishop of Utrecht, with the title, 'Compendiu[m] q[ui]dda[m] medici[n]ale Reyneri Oesterhusen dave[n]trie[n]sis utile curatori egrotanti Et volenti servare sanitatem'; f. 7r Johannes Behemensis, 'De institutione medici'; ff. 7r-8r: Three recipes in Latin for dishes from Cologne and a list of synonyms of plant names, with three names translated into Middle Dutch; ff. 8v-14v: Arnoldus de Villa Nova (b. c.1240, d. 1311) , 'Regimen sanitatis salernitanum' or 'Flos medicine', a collection of didactic verse on health, diet, and medicine put together for oral transmission by doctors at the school of Salerno, Italy, and assembled in written form in the 13th century, sometimes attributed to Johannes de Mediolano, here dated 'ao 1406 16 may' (f. 14v); ff. 15r-16r: Arnoldus de Villa Nova, 'T[ra]ctat[us] de laudibus virtutib[us] querci', a letter to Richard, Bishop of Canterbury (the rubric has 'Episcopum Cantuariensum', though there was no Archbishop of Canterbury named Richard during Villa Nova's life) about the medicinal properties of the oak tree; ff. 16v-20r: Arnoldus de Villa Nova: 'Tractatulus de vinis artificiatis'; ff. 20r-21r: Hippocrates: 'De signis mortis', with the heading, 'Incipit t[ra]ctatul[us] de d[er]tis moritutor[um] signis ypocratus'; ff. 22r-v: Two 16th-century recipes in Middle Dutch; ff. 23r-34v: Treatises in Middle Dutch with a Latin heading, 'De diversis coloribus, picturis et tincturis' (1506) (494-575); ff. 34v-115v Collectanea medica, a collection of medical texts from the 13th to 16th centuries, as follows: ff. 35v-37r: Alphabetical glossary of surgical terms in Middle Dutch; ff. 37r-38v: Medical and technical recipes in Middle Dutch (576-590); ff. 39r-46v: Collection of technical recipes with the Latin title, 'Incipiunt quedam dicta diuersaris artium et optima exercitia' (591-638); ff. 47r-52r: Collection of culinary recipes in Middle Dutch with the Latin heading, 'Incipiunt quedam dicta de diuersis confectis et sirupis et alijs materijs' (639-668), including recipes for gin (or brandy) with the heading, 'Gebrande wyn te maken' and the marginal rubric 'aqua vite' (ff. 51r-v); ff. 52r-65v: Medicinal waters or prescriptions, with the heading, 'Aqua philosophorum tegen dat grote ouel ende eyn tractat van allen medicinen vateren thoe maken' (669-768) and a table at the end (ff. 65r-v); ff. 66r-70r: 'Tractatulus de practica medicinae', a collection of extracts from Latin authors including Isidore, Constantinus, Pope Innocent III; ff. 70r-78v: Treatise on the treatment of wounds in Middle Dutch , with the Latin heading, 'Capitulum vi. et est tractatulus per se qualiter vulnera curari seu tractari debent' and dated at the end' 'Finis j.5.0.6. xv kl nouembris' attributed to the 'young Lanfranc' (of Milan); ff. 79r-83r: Latin - Middle Dutch botanical glossary; f. 83v: Latin - Middle Dutch glossary of names of illnesses, with the heading, 'Vocabula morborum'; ff. 83v-85r: Preparation and properties of medicinal waters, in Middle Dutch with the Latin heading, 'De virtutibus aquarum et de earum confectionibus tractatulus' (769-784); ff. 85r-86v: Recipes mainly for healing wounds, in Middle Dutch with the Latin heading, 'Sequuntur notabilia de Cirurgia' (785-801); ff. 86r-117r: Collection of medical recipes with the Latin heading, 'Libellus incipit de egritudibus a capite usque ad pedes' (802-1102), including a list of herbal remedies (1103-1213) with the rubric, Quomodo una herba sive res in medicinis pro alia mutari possit' (ff. 100r-102r); ff. 118r-127v: Johannes de Ketham, 'Chirurgia Parva'; ff. 128r-130r: Johannes de Ketham: 'Liber de matrice mulieris et impugnatione'; ff. 131r-136v: Joannes de Ketham, 'De diversis infirmitatibus et remediis earundem secundum alphabetum'; ff. 138r-141: Questions and answers on natural philosophy in Latin, with the rubric, 'Aliqua problemata in philosophia naturalia'; ff. 141r-v:

Opening screen on the British Library's entry
for Sloane MS345.

Collection of culinary recipes in Middle Dutch with the Latin heading 'Incip[i]unt quedam dicta de diuersis confectis et sirupis et alijs materijs' (639-668), including recipes for gin (or brandy) with the heading, 'Gebrande wyn te maken' the marginal rubric 'aqua vitae' (ff. 51r-v).[71]

However, Belgian historian Willy L. Braekman's translation of this 145-page Sloane compendium volume revealed that the said recipe—No. 666—described the making of 'one pot of brandy' that was distilled from 13 quarts of a mixture of ten quarts wine diluted with three quarts of beer.[72] The instructions offered the option of adding a handful of either sage leaves or a curious ingredient called *gorsbeyn of dameren* that was wrapped in a cloth bag and redistilled with the brandy.[73]

---

71. British Library, 'Sloane MS 345', <http://www.bl.uk/manuscripts/> [accessed 17 June 2016].

72. Various, *Medische En Technische Middelnederlandse Recepten*, ed. Willy L. Braekman (Ghent: Koninklijke Vlaamse Academie, 1975), 211-212.

73. Eric Van Schoonenberghe, 'Genever (gin): A Spirit Drink full of History, Science and Technology', *Sartonia*, 12 (1999), 99.

In other words, unlike von Schrick's description of *wachalterbeer wasser* or *cramatbeer wasser* and Brunschwig's notes on Water of Geniper berries', the Sloane compendium's *Gebrande wynte maken* recipe did not describe an intentional juniper berry spirit: It was a distillate optionally made with either sage or possibly juniper berries.

Van Schoonenberghe further noted that 'Gors is probably a corruption of the spelling of the words *ghurst*, *gurst*, or *guist* which in several Middle Dutch texts are synonymous with juniper and *beyn* can be read as *beyen* or berries.'[74] But, neither Braekman nor other linguistic scholars corroborate van Schoonenberghe's claim. To complicate matters further, there is another European evergreen shrub that bears a similar type of cone and needle-like leaves as juniper—common gorse. Can any light be shed by looking at similar words found in medieval English? The Oxford English Dictionary (OED) pointed to the word's usage in

---

74. Eric van Schoonenberghe, *Jenever in de Lage Landen* (Brugge: Stuchting Kunstboek, 1996), 49-50.

the *Saxon Leechdoms* in which the Old English phrase '*iuniperi pæt is gorst*' is noted.[75] With the aid of the ninth-century *Corpus Glossary* the OED continued to define the word *gorst* or *gors* as '1) The prickly shrub *Ulex europæus*; common furze, or whin [meaning gorse]; 2) juniper, n.'.[76] Finally, an entry in the 1879 edition of *The dictionary of English plant-names, Part I*, pointed to the word *gorst* as another term for *juniperus communis* or common juniper.[77] How did a ninth-century English term such as *gors* or *gorst* enter into the Middle Dutch lexicon and somehow be loosely linked to a language exchange that might have occurred during the twelfth and thirteenth centuries? Well, there were English wool traders who reached a com-

---

75. Oswald Cockaigne, *Leechdomes, Wortcunning, and Starcraft of Early England* (London: Longman, Green, Longman, Roberts, and Green, 1864), 72; Oxford English Dictionary, 'gorst, n.'

76. H. Sweet, 'Glossary (MS Cambridge, Corpus Christi College 144)', *The Oldest English Texts* (London : Published for the Early English Text Society by N. Trübner), 800; Oxford English Dictionary, 'gorse, n.'

77. James Britten and Robert Holland, *The dictionary of English plant-names, Part I* (London: Trübner & Co, 1886), 214.

mercial peak trading with the Flemish merchants around that time. Words could trickle into the Low Countries' lexicons. But that's a path for some other historians who specialise in early English language studies to ferret out.

The other recipe found in the Sloane compendium—No. 667—made *aqua vitæ* by distilling wine with nutmeg, ginger, galangal, grains of paradise, clove, cinnamon, and cardamom, then redistilling the spirit with crushed nutmeg, dried sage leaves, and cloves.[78] So you see, neither formula is a method for making either brandy nor gin as stated in the British Library's catalogue entry. And although these recipes are indeed early templates for spirits redistilled with botanicals which were not that common in the late fifteenth century, the library's dating of the compilation to circa 1500 raises a question about the alleged ages of these two recipes. This particular Sloane compendium

---

78.   Various, *Medische En Technische Middelnederlandse Recepten*, ed. Willy L. Braekman (Ghent: Koninklijke Vlaamse Academie, 1975), 211-212..

contains tracts ranging in date from as early as a 1260 copy of Arnaud de Villeneuve's *Tractatulus de vinis artificiatis* [A Treatise on Manufactured Wines] (ff. 20r-21r) and as late as a 1506 treatise titled *De diversis coloribus, picturis et tincturis* [About Different Colours, Paints, and Dyes] (ff. 34v-115v).[79] This makes van Schoonenberghe's claim to a 1495 origin to recipes Nos. 666 and 667 as questionable until the dates of the entire compendium's contents are verified forensically. (Historians, here's another challenge for you.) Finally, its relevance to the gin family tree is diminished even further since Puff von Schrick's description of a spirituous water distilled with juniper-berries predated this finding by twenty years!

We have to reiterate one more time here that our focus on alleged German or Dutch origins is not intended to marginalise the significance of the medieval juniper berry distillates developed and documented by Italian alchemist Alexius Ruscello Pedemontanus in his 1555 book *De' secreti*

---

79. British Library: Sloane MS345, ff. 20r-21r and ff. 34v-115v.

del reuerendo donno Alessio Piemontese [Secrets of the Reverend Don Alessio Piedmonte] and Polish physician Stefan Falimirz's 1534 volume *O ziolach y o moczy gich* [About herbs and urine].[80]

But there is no evidence of a direct connection between these landmark alchemical works and early modern English distillation. The use of juniper berries in a wide variety of medical applications is found throughout medieval and early modern England and Europe, such as:

> ...resisting the Plague and venomous Beasts, opens the Urinary Passage and Stomach, curing shortness of Breath, Drops, Consumption, Convulsion, Pain in the Belly and Side, Rupture, gives speedy Delivery [to women in labour], strengthens the Memory, clears the Sight, comforts the Brain, cureth Gout, Scurvy, Leprosy, Scab, Itch, and Piles; all this,

---

80.   Alexius Ruscello Pedemontanus, *De' secreti del reuerendo donno Alessio Piemontese, prima parte, diuisa in sei libri* (Venice: Sigismondo Bordogna, 1555); Stefan Falimirz, *O ziolach y o moczy gich* (Krakow: Floria Ungler, 1534).

and more, it performs by taking the Berries powder'd in Wine.[81]

So, it stands to reason medicinal and culinary recipes containing juniper berries flourished wherever juniper trees grew, especially in an era punctuated by recurring pandemics of the bubonic plague. Our sights, however, are firmly cast solely on the origin of an English juniper berry spirit and its relevance to English gin's development. Consequently, this early stepping stone from commercially printed German distillation books and their English translation allows us to now look at their importance to the emergence of distilling by English housewives.

---

81.   Anonymous, *An English Herbal, or, A discovery of the physical vertues of all herbs in this Kingdom* (London: A. Cloners], 1690), 40.

CHAPTER THREE

'...are also SKILFUL in surgery and DISTILLATION OF waters'[82]

The printing press made distillation books collectively outsell the Bible, while the English royal court set a new trend, drinking spirits instead of just wines and beers.

L IKE THEIR GERMAN counterparts, English housewives quickly adopted the practice of distilling spirits. It happened for a surprising reason. Shortly after its appearance on English shores—through Roger Bacon and other English alchemists—distillation became

---

82.   William Harrison, *The Description of England: The Classic Contemporary Account of Tudor Social Life,* ed. by Georges Edelen (New York: Dover Publications, Inc., 1994), 228-229.

vital for producing medicines. However, only the wealthy could afford to be treated by physicians in medieval and early modern England. Healers who were not licenced medical practitioners were in demand largely because they charged little or nothing to minister treatment unlike their professional cohorts.[83] It was common for women to treat the sick with herbs and potions. In addition, there were monks who administered medical aid to travellers and the poor (as dramatised in the mid-1990s British TV series *Cadfael*, starring Derek Jacobi). There were also apothecaries who prepared and sold medicinal compounds made from herbs and spices, and treated patients without any formal medical training or qualification charging far less for their services than physicians.

Apothecaries who plied their trade in London were monitored by the Worshipful Company

83.   William L. Minkowski, 'Women Healers of the Middle Ages: Selected Aspects of Their History', *American Journal of Public Health*, 82/2 (1992), 293.

of Grocers which was incorporated in 1428.[84] Many of the Company's members had shops on Bucklesbury Street 'where they stored and sold spices, confectionery, perfumes, spiced wines, herbs and drugs which they compounded and dispensed to the public'.[85] Next, let's meet the women mentioned above who also filled this healthcare gap, practising vernacular medicine—any healing process that employed herbal remedies. They plied their distilling and compounding knowledge at home from their kitchens, treating their families, friends, and neighbours. Physician William L. Minkowski noted that: 'In England, before King Henry V's decree of 1421, ordering a ban on women practitioners of medicine and surgery, female doctors and surgeons were less threatened by their male colleagues.'[86] Yes, female healers were that

---

84.   Worshipful Society of Apothecaries, 'Origins', <https://www.apothecaries.org/history/> [accessed 3 May 2020].

85.   Worshipful Society of Apothecaries, 'Origins', <https://www.apothecaries.org/history/> [accessed 3 May 2020].

86.   William L. Minkowski, 'Women Healers of the Middle Ages: Selected Aspects of Their History', *American Journal of Public Health*, 82/2 (1992), 293; Great Britain, 'A Petition to the Parliament of 1421 for Protective Legislation', *Rotuli Parliamentorum*, Vol. 4, ed. by J. Strachey, et al. (London: HMSO, 1767-77), 158.

numerous and that unregulated. Medieval English literature professor Diane Watt pointed out that the letters written by Margaret Paston and other female members of the Paston family in the late fifteenth-century offered evidence that 'women within the late medieval household continued to play important roles when it came to healing as well as caring for the sick', from 'nursing to treating ailments and to prescribing and dispensing medicines'.[87] Sixteenth-century cleric William Harrison alluded to the distilling skills of the ladies of the English royal court, extolling that: 'How many of the eldest sort are also skilful in surgery and distillation of waters beside and other artificial practices.'[88] And historian Constance Anne Wilson concluded that while ladies of the house practised distilling regardless of household size, 'In larger aristocratic households, ...distill-

---

87.   Diane Watt, 'Mary the Physician: Women, Religion and Medicine in the Middle Ages', *Medicine, Religion and Gender in Medieval Culture*, ed. by N. Yoshikawa (Martlesham, Suffolk: Boydell & Brewer, 2015), 39.

88.   William Harrison, *The Description of England: The Classic Contemporary Account of Tudor Social Life*, ed. by Georges Edelen (New York: Dover Publications, Inc., 1994), 228-229.

ing duties were assigned to one or two servants.'[89] That's a lot of high-born women playing doctor and distiller in one capacity or another.

This raises the question: How did English women learn how to distil? Did they learn from the local monks? They obviously shared recipes like any good housewife would as a sisterly or neighbourly gesture. But what was their literacy level if they learned or sharpened their skills by reading the new crop of printed books on distillation? Recent interest in historian David Cressy's 1977 study of the reading and writing ability of the early modern English female population has garnered intriguing new conclusions by historian Eleanor Hubbard.[90] Concentrating on the female population of sixteenth- and seventeenth-century London, in particular, Hubbard determined that social status affected literacy greatly. Her research

---

89.   Constance Anne Wilson, *Water of Life: A History of Wine-Distilling and Spirits 500 BC to AD 2000* (Totnes, Devon: Prospect Books, 2006), 169.

90.   David Cressy, 'Levels of Illiteracy in England 1530-1730', The Historical Journal, 20/1 (1977), 1-23; Eleanor Hubbard, 'Reading, Writing, and Initiating Female Literacy in Early Modern London', *Journal of British Studies*, 54/3 (2015), 553-577.

demonstrated that 73 per cent of gentlemen's and esquires' wives were literate, and 30 per cent of the spouses of merchants and tradesmen could read as well. There was even a literacy rate of 23 per cent was found amongst artisans' wives. This suggests that about three-quarters of London's aristocratic women, and later, middling-sort and artisan housewives joined their ranks, gleaning tips from a virtual flood of advice manuals. They learned how to distil because they could read books. Add to this the ability to keep journals of their recipes and to share their findings in letters written to other women. (A future path for research by historians could determine how many early-modern English women in rural areas across all social strata also possessed basic reading and writing skills which could open this level of enquiry even further.) Consequently, urban and rural women had access to the new advice manuals thanks to the rise in female literacy during the sixteenth and seventeenth centuries. But what tools did they use to manufacture distillates?

Stillatories (that's what they were originally called) were mentioned as early as the late fourteenth century. One instance appeared in Geoffrey Chaucer's *Canterbury Tales* (1387-1400) in 'The Canon's Yeoman's Prologue':

> His forehead dropped as a stillatorie
> Were ful of plantayne and of pari-
> torie[91]

This can be translated into modern English to mean that his forehead dripped sweat like drops from a still, smelling of plantain and pellitory herbs.

Stillatories were crafted in all shapes and sizes—designs that stood the test of time for centuries.[92] Fashioned from clay or even glass, a simple base or a 'cucurbit'—a gourd-like vessel—contained the liquid and solid materials to be dis-

---

91.   Geoffrey Chaucer, '8.2 The Canon's Yeoman's Prologue', lines 580-581, https://chaucer.fas.harvard.edu/pages/canons-yeomans-prologue-and-tale [accessed 10 January 2023].

92.   Trish Hayward and Peter Hayward, 'Pewter Stills', in *Journal of the Pewter Society*, Autumn 2013, 4.

tilled.[93] Stillatories—or simply, stills—were as rudimentary as the brewing tools found in both large and small English households. The simplest form of these was the cold still.[94]

The base was secured with a conical or dome-like head that allowed vapours to rise and circulate inside the dome which was wrapped in a wet cloth to keep it cool before the steam streamed down the bec or the nose into a receiving vessel. The base and head were balanced above a furnace, a dish of smouldering charcoal, or set into a balneo or balneum marie, which was a water bath set over a furnace that allowed the liquid to distil without overheating.

A large balneo could accommodate multiple stills so production could be increased efficiently. Cold distillation was a slow process, but it

---

93. Trish Hayward and Peter Hayward, 'Pewter Stills', in *Journal of the Pewter Society*, Autumn 2013, 5. Evidence of glass stillatories have been identified in archaeological excavations in English monasteries and one report mentions Henry VI's Master of Stillatories Robert Broke benefitted from using glass instead clay stills. (See Andre Simon, 'The Art of Distillation', lecture delivered at The Vintner's Hall by the Wine Trade Club, 1912.)

94. Constance Anne Wilson, *Water of Life: A History of Wine-Distilling and Spirits 500 BC to AD 2000* (Totnes, Devon: Prospect Books, 2006), 197.

One form of cold still from Dr John French's The Art of Distillation. *(above) and a glass gourd still with head from Dr John French's* The Art of Distillation *(below) (Source: private collection).*

A balneos depicted with multiple disitllationsfrom Dr John French's The Art of Distillation. *(above) and a glass gourd still with head from Dr John French's* The Art of Distillation *(below) (Source: private collection).*

Multiple glass stills and furnaces linked together from Dr John French's The Art of Distillation *(Source: private collection).*

worked well for extracting essences for medicines and floral waters. Women also produced small quantities of *eau-de-vie*—a spirit extracted from cherries or mint or other fruits and botanicals—with cold stills.[95] One variation of the cold still was called a retort, which was fashioned from glass as a one-piece unit. This design could be joined in multiples in a cascade formation if repeated distillation was desired.[96] Of course, domestic distillation's value for medicinal applications did not go unnoticed by the government. Parliament essentially legitimised the practice of vernacular medi-

---

95. Constance Anne Wilson, *Water of Life: A History of Wine-Distilling and Spirits 500 BC to AD 2000* (Totnes, Devon: Prospect Books, 2006), 206.

96. Trish Hayward and Peter Hayward, 'Pewter Stills', in *Journal of the Pewter Society*, Autumn 2013, 5.

cine, on 12 May 1543, with the passage of *An Act that Persons being no common Surgeons, may administer outward Medicines.*[97] The statute permitted anyone with a working knowledge of 'herbs, roots, and waters or the operation of same' to treat patients with 'any... herbs, ointments, baths, poultices and plasters, according to their cunning, experience, and knowledge'.[98] (The word 'waters' used in this context implied that the liquids were either alcoholic distillates or non-alcoholic hydrosols.) Thus, with this governmental benediction, apothecaries treated the afflicted with any remedy they deemed fit. And by its wording, Parliament inadvertently granted permission not only to apothecaries but to housewives and gentlewomen who, as part of their domestic role, were expected 'to keep herb gardens, compound remedies, and treat the illnesses and injuries of their families and

---

97.   34 & 35 Henry VIII, c.8,9.
98.   34 & 35 Henry VIII, c.8,9.

neighbours' plus by inference expected to distil medicinal spirits and hydrosols.[99]

This demand for vernacular medicine was not limited to households in the countryside. An historian who specialised in the study of early modern English medical practitioners who treated the poor and lower sorts, Margaret Pelling, and medical historian Charles Webster, determined that by 1600, London's population of 200,000 had one medical professional to treat every 400 Londoners. [100] (At the time of this writing, there are 3.2 physicians for every thousand citizens in the UK.[101]) So, apothecaries and housewives were as much a necessity as physicians to administer care to London's sick. Early-modern historians

99.   Lucinda M. Beier, *Sufferers and Healers: The Experience of Illiness in Seventeenth-Century England* (London: Routledge and Kegan Paul, 1987), 29.

100.   Margaret Pelling and Charles Webster, 'Medical Practitioners', *Health, Medicine and Mortality in the Sixteenth Century*, ed. by Charles Webster (Cambridge: Cambridge University Press, 1979), 165-236; Anthony Wrigley, 'Urban Growth and Agricultural Change: England and the Continent in the Early Modern Period,' *The Journal of Interdisciplinary History*, 15/4 (Spring 1985), 638-672.

101.   World Data Bank, 'Physicians (per 1,000 people) - United Kingdom' <https://data.worldbank.org/indicator/> [accessed 21 February 2024].

Katherine A. Allen and Anne Stobart deduced that distilled and compounded medicines formed a 'charitable provision for the poor [which] has been portrayed initially as a source of confirmation of piety for wealthy women.'[102] Furthermore, home distillation offered middling-sort housewives an opportunity to emulate their aristocratic superiors. Middling sorts. Who were the middling sorts? The sixteenth and seventeenth centuries saw the emergence of a new social group called the middling sorts. This economic group earned more than their lessers—artisans, labourers, and of course, the poor. They aspired to emulate the lifestyle of the aristocracy just like the yuppies of the 1980s.

But it was the drinking culture of the English royal court that helped transform distillates into pleasurable potables—not just medicines—inspiring the gentry and the middling sorts to

102.   Katherine J. Allen, 'Manuscript Recipe Collections and Elite Domestic Medicine in Eighteenth-Century England' (unpublished thesis, University of Oxford, 2015), 19; Anne Stobart, 'The Making of Domestic Medicine: Gender, Self-Help and Therapeutic Determination in Household Healthcare in South-West England in the Late Seventeenth Century' (unpublished thesis, Middlesex University, 2008), 32.

adopt this new trend. Economic and social historian John Chartres noted that the 'consumption of distilled liquors as beverages in England dates only from the later sixteenth century'.[103] Yet Constance Anne Wilson concluded that the social consumption of spirits was introduced into the English royal court's drinking culture by the mid-sixteenth century, noting that Henry VIII replaced hippocras—a wine infused with botanicals—with *aqua vitæ* in his royal court.[104] As we mentioned before, in Scotland, *aqua vitæ* was the name ascribed to all ardent spirits. But in England and Ireland, *aqua vitæ* was a term that described spirits redistilled or rectified with a base spirit

---

103. John Chartres, 'No English Calvados? English distillers and the cider industry in the seventeenth and eighteenth centuries?', *English rural society 1500-1800: Essays in honour of Joan Thirsk*, ed. by John Chartres and David Hey (Cambridge: Cambridge University Press, 1990).

104. Constance Anne Wilson, *Water of Life: A History of Wine-Distilling and Spirits 500 BC to AD 2000* (Totnes, Devon: Prospect Books, 2006), 177. Hippocras was a common cordial consumed by royalty and the aristocracy in fifteenth-century England. For example, apothecary to Edward IV, John Clerk, supplied Katherine Neville, the Duchess of Norfolk with hippocras by the gallon between 1463 and 1471. (see Hannes Kleineke, 'The medicines of Katherine, Duchess of Norfolk 1463-1471', *Medical History*, 59/4 (2015), 520.)

and a blend of botanicals.[105] The trend for these more complex liquors became more apparent by the late fifteenth century during the Tudor dynasty.

Wilson noted that during Elizabeth I's reign another spirit—*aqua rosa solis*—was popularly consumed as a digestif and was even promoted as an aphrodisiac. Also known as rosolio, this drink was often said to have originated in the city of Turin and the Piedmonte region of Italy. The English version of *aqua rosa solis* involved steeping Sundew flowers (*Drosera rotundifolia L.*) and *aqua compositæ*—a rectified spirit like *aqua vitæ*—for twenty days with a blend of fruits, spices, and flowers.[106] The mixture was then filtered, sweetened with sugar, then tinted with gum amber, fine gold leaf, plus powdered pearl and coral.

6. Rose-Solis

Take the hearbe Rosa Solis, gath-

---

105.   Constance Anne Wilson, *Water of Life: A History of Wine-Distilling and Spirits 500 BC to AD 2000* (Totnes, Devon: Prospect Books, 2006), 150.

106.   Constance Anne Wilson, *Water of Life: A History of Wine-Distilling and Spirits 500 BC to AD 2000* (Totnes, Devon: Prospect Books, 2006), 179; Hugh Plat, *Delightes for Ladies, to Adorne Their Persons, Tables, Closets, and Distillatories* (London: Peter Short, 1602), b6.

ered in July one gallon, picke out
all the black moats fro the leaues,
of dates halfe a pound, Cinamon,
Ginger, cloues of each one ounce,
grains half an ounce, fine sugar a
pound and a halfe, red Rose leaues,
green or dried foure handfuls, stiepe
all these in a gallon of good Aqua
composita in a glasse close stopped
wit waxe during twentie daies, shake
it wel together once euvery two
daies. Your sugar must be pudered,
your spices brused onely or gros-
sely beaten, your dates cut in long
slices the stones taken away. If you
adde two or three grains of Amber-
greece, and as much muske in your
glasse amonst the rest of the ingredients, it will haue a pleasant smel.
Some adde the gum aber with corall and pearle finely poudered, and
fine leafe golde. Some vse to boile
Ferdinando bucke in Rosewater, til
thy huve purchased a faire deepe
crimson colour, & when the same

is cold they colour their Rose Solis
and Aqua Rubea therewith.[107]

Elizabeth I's own appreciation for social spirits consumption and for spirits' medicinal value is further evidenced by the monopoly she granted in 1596—a plague year—to courtier and Groom of the Privy Chamber Richard Drake and his partner Michael Stanhope to licence all distilleries in and around London for the manufacture of both *aqua compositæ* and *aqua vitæ* for a period of 21 years.[108] Generally speaking, recipes for *aqua compositæ* macerated more than a dozen botanicals in wine for about twelve hours. This infusion was

107.   Hugh Plat, *Delightes for Ladies, to Adorne Their Persons, Tables, Closets, and Distillatories* (London: Peter Short, 1602), b6. This recipe serves only as an example of a *rosa solis* produced during the 1590s and early 1600s.

108.   Sir Simonds D'Ewes and Paul Bowes, 'The Journal of the House of Commons', *The Journals of all the Parliaments During the Reign of Queen Elizabeth: Both of the House of Lords and the House of Commons* (London: John Starkey, 1682), 650; J.C. Drummond and Anne Wilbreham, *The Englishman's Food: Five Centuries of English Diet* (London: Jonathan Cape, 1939, revised 1957), 115; George Unwin, *The Gilds and Companies of London*, Fourth ed. (London: Frank Case & Company, 1963), 297; Jessica Warner, *Craze: Gin and Debauchery in an Age of Reason* (London: Profile Book, 2004), 25-26; John Chartres, 'No English Calvados? English distillers and the cider industry in the seventeenth and eighteenth centuries?', *English rural society 1500-1800: Essays in honour of Joan Thirsk*, ed. by John Chartres and David Hey (Cambridge: Cambridge University Press, 1990), 314-315.

distilled in a pewter alembic, which could have referred to either a head still or hot still fashioned from pewter. Production instructions noted to keep 'the first cleare water that cometh by itself, & so likewise the second' so that the final liquid produced a pint of 'the better sort' finished spirit.[109]

8. D. Steuens aqua composita

Take a gallo of gascascoign wine, of giner, galingale, cinamon, nutmegs & grains, Annis seeds, fennell seedes and caraway seeds, of each a dram, of Sage, Mints, red Roses, Time, Pellitory, Rosemarie, wil thyme, camomil, lauender, of each a handful, bray the spices small and bruse the berbes, letting them macerate 12. Hours stirring it nowe and then, then distill by a llimbecke of pewter, keeping the firs cleere water that commeth by itself, and so likewide the second. You shall draw much about a pinte

---

109.   Hugh Plat, *Delightes for Ladies, to Adorne Their Persons, Tables, Closets, and Distillatories* (London: Peter Short, 1602), b8.

of the better sorte from euery gallon of wine.[110]

While the monopoly's stated purpose was to eliminate the production of 'unwholesome spirits' and the 'temptation to produce 'prophy-lactic "plague waters" from hogwash and dregs', it also facilitated the distillation of spirits for a growing audience of social drinkers.[111] Looking at the recipes for *rosa solis* and *aqua compositæ*, you can see a change in the types of spirits produced in England. Rather than simply extracting spirit from wine or beer or producing a spirit that was distilled from the infusion of a single botanical, more complex formulations were introduced into early modern English drinking culture.

Spirits consumption continued to insinu-ate itself into the fabric of the English royal court's social activities when, in 1603, James I ascended

110.   Hugh Plat, *Delightes for Ladies, to Adorne Their Persons, Tables, Closets, and Distillatories* (London: Peter Short, 1602), b6. This recipe serves only as an example of a Dr Stevens Aqua Composita produced during the 1590s and early 1600s—of which there were many published during the period.

111.   John Strype, *A Survey of the Cities of London and Westminster*, Book V (London: 1598, reprinted J.M. Dent & Sons, Ltd., 1720), 236-237.

to the throne. His wife Anne of Denmark imported the Danish royal court's drinking habits, which highlighted spirits consumption, to her new English home.[112] From this royal launch point, the social pastime of spirits consumption trickled down and was assimilated into the aspiring middling-sort English social drinking culture.[113]

'...approved and used with great and marvellous success'[114]

THE PRINTING REVOLUTION in Germany sparked a rise in domestic and commercial distillation and the same transpired in England, where 153 printed advice manuals filled with distillation recipes tweaked

---

112.   P. Vandyke Price, *The Penguin Book of Spirits and Liqueurs* (Harmondsworth, 1980), 205; Constance Anne Wilson, *Water of Life: A History of Wine-Distilling and Spirits 500 BC to AD 2000* (Totnes, Devon: Prospect Books, 2006), 195.

113.   B. Ann Tlusty, 'Water of Life, Water of Death: The Controversy over Brandy and Gin in Early Modern Augsburg,' *Central European History*, 31/1 (1998), 5.

114.   B. Ann Tlusty, 'Water of Life, Water of Death: The Controversy over Brandy and Gin in Early Modern Augsburg,' *Central European History*, 31/1 (1998), 128.

the interest of an equally enthusiastic audience. Between 1527 and 1605, about 400,000 copies were printed and sold through the emerging printing and bookselling trades.[115] London's book trade in the sixteenth century was represented by about 24 printing houses which were mostly located around the old St Paul's churchyard, Holborn, and Aldersgate.[116] This trade was monitored by the Worshipful Company of Stationers, which was organised in 1403 and was granted a monopoly a century later, in 1503, thus regulating England's burgeoning information revolution. John Day was one of those London printers who, in 1565, published another bestselling distillation book which was originally written by Swiss physician Conrad Gessner and translated into English

115.   Paul Slack, 'Mirrors of Health and Treasures of Poor Men: The Uses of the Vernacular Medical Literature of Tudor England,' in *Health, Medicine and Mortality in the Sixteen Century*, ed. by Charles Webster (Cambridge: Cambridge University Press, 1979), 238-239.

116.   Stationers Company, 'Tradition and Heritage', <https://ww.stationers.org/> [accessed 6 February 2022]; British Library, 'Shakespeare in print: 1. London book trade', <https://www.bl.uk/treasures/> [accessed 6 February 2022].

by Oxford scholar Peter Morwen.[117] Titled *A new booke of distillatyon of waters, called the Treasure of Euonymus*, the compilation included distillation recipes attributed to alchemists Roger Bacon, Albertus Magnus, Geber, Avicenna, Hieronymous Brunschwig, amongst other, more diverse sources. For example, one chapter titled 'Aqua vitæ against pestilence approved and used with great and marvellous success by a certayn physician of our tyme Solodrun in Helutia the yere of our Lord 1547' contained a very complicated recipe for 'A most noble water of vertues' derived from a 'certayne written boke.'[118] The ambiguous explanation of the recipe's source is accentuated by the improbable list of ingredients and the recipe's execution. Aside from the infusion of about 50 minerals and botanicals in wine for fourteen days, the steps to distillation and ageing deep in a cellar before additional dis-

---

117.   Conrad Gessner and Peter Morwen, *A New Booke of Destillatyon of Waters, Called the Treasure of Euonymus* (London: John Day, 1565), passim.

118.   Conrad Gessner and Peter Morwen, *A New Booke of Destillatyon of Waters, Called the Treasure of Euonymus* (London: John Day, 1565), 128.

tillation was conducted, make the formula appear
more contrived than authentic.

Take the best perles, Hyacinth of the
east, mother of perles, corall whyte
and read, of euery one.ii.ounces,
halfe an ounce of the horne of an
unicorn, saffron, mirhe, Boliarmon,
terræ tigillatæ, zedoriæ, Venetæ,
wode of aloes, euory, Mithra datii,
triacle of Alexandria, chosen cinnamon ben white and red, the barke
of a citron and the sedes of euvry
one an ounce & a half. The little
bones of y harte of a hart. Xii. Of
them, the kirnels of peony, berries
of iuniper, of ether.xl. Conferrue
of buglos. li.ounces. The tormen-
til, common diotani, inulæ, aftrantia,
selandine, common Lybistici, mor-
sus diaboli, ari, Valeriane, that kind
of Sarifrage whiche the German
call bibinel, anglica of the rotes of
euerye one of the hearbes. ii.ounces.
Sage, Scaboius, Rew, wild mint, peny
royall, the les centauri, Wormwode,
white Rooses and Red, of euerye
one a handful. Liquors distilled of
Rosemary, Gentian, Melissa or bau-

line, Certain wild Roses, sochoes
or cicerbita, called sowithittle, hys-
sop, floures of Burrage, bigger
plantain, floure Deluice, or eueryone. v.ounces These thus gathered
together, take the liquors of them
destilled in Balneo Marie according-
lye, and mingle them with the best
old Elseter wine, or rather with. liii.
Poundes of Aqua vitæ. Vi. Times destilled then pout them in a stronge
cucurbita of glasses, that wil hold.
iiii. Good ale quarters which thoou
shalt claye well and let it stande in
Balneo Marie. liii. Daies. Afterwarde,
then though shalt burnt the hyacinc-
tes, coralles, pearles and mother of
perles into pouder, as men do lim &
grind them upon marble diligently,
til thou canst tele no roughnes in
the pouder. Put thys pouder into
some vessel, and make it with Rose
water into a liquor, & what so euer
remaineth sharp or rough, which is
not mist with the water, grinde it
again, and wash it the second time.
A man maye resolue the coralles
into water when they are once
pund or ground, setting them in the

juice of Berberies, which way is better then the other. After this beat the rotes meanly and likewise the sedes of the iuniper and pæony the herbes thou shalt cut. Afterwarde put the herbes, rotes, and precious stones moistened and made liquid with the Rose water, into a strong glasen cucurbita that will hold sixe great ale quartes, there about. I ges. vi. Dutche mooses to be, which I thinck meanth by Mesuras, and pour upon them the Aqua vitæ which is digested with the destilled liquors in Balneo Marie, and when the curcubita is defnded & closed round about with clay of wisdom, put it into a put digged in a moyst place, as in som celler under the earth. li. cubits diep, iiii cubits or there aboute wide and log, which thou shalt fil with hors dug and lime strawed and laid by courses, now one laier of the one, now an other of the other, til it be. li. fote about the pit. In the midst hereof thouse shalt let the cucurbita stand for a monthe, then take the dung away by little and little : and the matter which it conteineth to be destilled, thou shale distribute it into. vi. Les cucurbitas, and destil them in Balneo Marie, with so llow a fire, that from the falling of one drop, till the falling of an other, though maistee tell one, ii. iii. iiii. till thou come at ten. For thou must in any wise, take hede that the be not to hot, whe the distillation is once ended, stur the dregs that be left in euery one of the cucurbitas with a sticke moderately, and poure the water that is drawne oute of them in againe, and destill them again with a slow fire as before. When this destillacion is once ended, pour out the dregs and distribute the liquors, gaterd in vi cucurbits into ii cucurbits, of iii greate ale quartes a pece, and destill them in Balneo Marie gentleye.[119]

Another chapter offered a more functional formula for *aqua vitæ*, and claimed it was pro-

---

119.   Conrad Gessner and Peter Morwen, *A New Booke of Destillatyon of Waters, Called the Treasure of Euonymus* (London: John Day, 1565), 128.

duced at the Emperor's Court at Constantinople.[120]
Infusing 27 botanicals in wine with nuts, fruit
seeds, and sweetener for five days, the mixture
was then distilled and administered to 'confirmeth
the stomack, cheareth the mind, and remedieth
the disease called gutta, the drop, the agewe, the
coughe, the wombe, and the wormes in the head.'

> Cloues, Nutmegges, ginger, Cori-
> ander, Galingall, long peper, iuni-
> perberries, Arantia, sage, Basilicus,
> Roosemary, Amaracus, Mint, Lettis,
> bay leaves, peny royall, Gentia, the
> flours of Sambucus or elder, white
> Rooses, spikenard, wode of Aloes,
> cardomum, Mugwort, of euery like
> much. A Pomgranate, ii figs, Passule,
> almons, dates, of euerye one a little.
> When these are pund, mixt a part
> of hony and sugar. Stiepe them al
> I good wine v daies & destil them.
> That is the best liquor that runs out

---

120.   Conrad Gessner and Peter Morwen, *A New Booke of Destillatyon of Waters, Called the Treasure of Euonymus* (London: John
Day, 1565), 161-162.

first the next is weaker & the 3 the weakest. ...[121]

In the chapter of 'divers kindes of Aqua vitæ composed', there was another remedy for the pestilence that macerated 50 botanicals, including lavender flowers, wormwood, juniper berries, angelica, rhubarb, the bark of citron, saffron, and cinnamon into wine which was then distilled 'in a limbeck [alembic].'[122] What made this recipe different from the Solodrun in Helutia spirit narrated earlier is that the production process was far simpler and believable.

An Aqua vitæ against the pestilence.

Take Rewe, Sage, the flowers of Lavendule, Maiora, Wormwood, Rosemary, red Roses, blessed thistle, pimpernel, Tormentii valerian, berryes of Juniper, berrues of baies, terræ sigil. (that is ground sill) bole armoniack

---

121.   Conrad Gessner and Peter Morwen, *A New Booke of Destillatyon of Waters, Called the Treasure of Euonymus* (London: John Day, 1565), 160-161.

122.   Conrad Gessner and Peter Morwen, *A New Booke of Destillatyon of Waters, Called the Treasure of Euonymus* (London: John Day, 1565), 127-128.

preared, of eueryone two drammes.
Dictamni, angelica, bistorra, the bark
of citron, melissa, commonly called
baulm, zedoaria, inulæ cam, gentian,
thaponticum or century, of eueryone three drames. Coriander prepared, flowers of borage, buglose,
sandal or lauders whyte and red,
the sede of correl, basil, rewbarbe,
ben white and red, the graines of
paradise, peper, of eueryone a dram
and a halfe: ginger two drammes.
Cinamon, saffrom, spyces of con-
fections against pestilence, elec-
tuarii liberates, lectuarii of precious
stones, diamosehi is swete, dicam-
eron diamber, diarhodon abbatis,
lætificantis Almanforis, of euery one
a dram. Calami arom, egloflowers,
maces, nutmeggs, cubebarum, car-
domomi, glaingall, agallochl of euery
two scrup. The bone of a hart, spike-
nard, camphora, of euery one halfe
a dram, eighte leaues of gold, halfe
a scrup of masch; shosen triable. liii
ounes. Michritlatti two onces. Sub-

limated and   rectified wyne two
quarters. Destill them in a limbeck.[123]

All the *Treasure of Euonymous* recipes
involved rectifying multiple botanicals, including
juniper berries in some. They reinforce the sug-
gestion that English *aqua vitæ* made with a blend
of botanicals had become fashionable and that
early modern English distillation achieved a new
level of sophistication that transcended the simple
extraction of spirit from wine, fermented grains,
or beer. What we cannot confirm is that any real
human being—let alone an aspiring distiller—ever
produced Gessner's recipes with any level of success. But it can be said that these printed formulas
got the creative juices flowing in many an amateur
and budding commercial distiller.

The seventeenth century saw English
domestic distillation evolve rapidly thanks to this
proliferation of advice manuals combined with a
few technological advancements in still design.
First published, in 1602, by printer Peter Short,

---

123.   Conrad Gessner and Peter Morwen, *A New Booke of Destillatyon of Waters, Called the Treasure of Euonymus* (London: John
Day, 1565), 127-128.

Hugh Plat's *Delightes for Ladies* was a bestseller, with subsequent editions produced in 1608, 1609, and 1618.[124] The son of prominent London brewer Richard Plat, who operated the Old Swan brewery on Jones Street, Hugh Plat was a brewer by heritage and an armchair intellectual who pursued knowledge through reading, observation, and experimentation, although he had no known experience in the commercial application of this information. In this slim volume, he introduced three recipes that are pertinent to our discussion. First, the 'Dr Stevens' Aqua Composita' described earlier (see page 90) was the base spirit used to produce Elizabeth I's *aqua rosa solis* (see page 87) and one of the first spirits commercially produced under the monopoly granted by Queen Elizabeth I to Richard Drake.[125]

Plat's second spirit recipe of interest was usquebaugh, which he alternately called Irish *aqua*

---

124.   Hugh Plat, *Delightes for Ladies, to Adorne Their Persons, Tables, Closets, and Distillatories* (London: Peter Short, 1602), passim.

125.   Hugh Plat, *Delightes for Ladies, to Adorne Their Persons, Tables, Closets, and Distillatories* (London: Peter Short, 1602), b8.

vitæ.[126] This formula macerated a rectified *aqua compositæ* (see page 90) for five or six days with liquorice root plus anise seeds. The infusion was then fined—or allowed to become clear for another three or four days—then sweetened with molasses. Finally, it was dulcified for a second time with dates and raisins.

9. Vsquebath, or Irish aquavitæ

To euery gallon of good Aqua compositæ, put two ounces of chosen liquerice bruised, and cast into small pieces, but first clensed from all his filth, and two ounces of Annis seeds that are cleane & bruised, let them macerate fiue or sixe days in a wooden vessel, stopping the same close, and then drawe as much as will runne cleare, dissouing in that cleare Aqua vitæ fiue or sixe spoonefuls of the best Malassoes you can get, Spanish cute if you can get it, is thought better then Malaosses, then put this into another vessel; and after three or

---

126.   Hugh Plat, *Delightes for Ladies, to Adorne Their Persons, Tables, Closets, and Distillatories* (London: Peter Short, 1602), b9.

foure days (the more the better)
when the liquor hath fined it selfe,
you may vse the same: some adde
Dates and Rasons for the sunne to
their receipt; those grounds which
remain you may redistill and make
more Aqua composita of them, and
of that Aqua composita, you may
make more Vsque-bath.[127]

Usquebaugh was very popular according
to contemporary reports. Author of a European
travelogue Fynes Moryson recounted, in 1617, that:
'The Irish Aquavitæ, vulgarly called Vsqubaugh,
is held the best in the World of that kind; which
is also made ine *England*, but nothing so good as
that which is brought out of Ireland.'[128] He justi-
fied his preference on the inclusion of raisins,
fennel seeds, and 'other things' that reduced the
alcoholic heat on the imbiber's palate. This suggests English *aqua vitæ* was more herbal in nature
and less sweet than Irish *aqua vitæ* or usquebaugh.

---

127.   Hugh Plat, *Delightes for Ladies, to Adorne Their Persons, Tables, Closets, and Distillatories* (London: Peter Short, 1602), b9.

128.   Fynes Moryson, *Itinerary; Book III*, Glasgow edition, volume IV (1908), 196-198.

Moryson then added that this 'English-Irish' drink appealed to both sexes who 'vse excesse therein'. While Moryson lends only a singular perspective on the gender balance of seventeenth-century consumers of alcohol, it invites further research by historians into the level of spirits production and consumption by both sexes in early modern England and Ireland.

It should be noted that this category of complex formulae known collectively as usquebaugh is also the etymological parent of the term 'whisky' which first appeared around 1728. However, these recipes share much more in common with modern gin.[129]

The third and final distillate of note in Plat's book—Spirit of Spices—rectified a wine spirit or brandy with oils instead of raw or dry botanicals.[130] Aged in a closed container for one

---

129.   Oxford English Dictionary, 'whisky', n.1. Short for whisky-bae, etc. (Gaelic uisgebeatha lit. 'water of life'), though this is not actually evidenced so early (but Ramsay has usque for usquebaugh n., in 1728). In modern trade usage, Scotch whisky and Irish whiskey are thus distinguished in spelling; whisky is the usual spelling in Britain and whiskey that in the U.S.

130.   Hugh Plat, *Delightes for Ladies, to Adorne Their Persons, Tables, Closets, and Distillatories* (London: Peter Short, 1602), b3.

month, Plat concluded that this liquid was 'a most delicate Spirite of each of the saide aromaticall bodies.'[131]

3. Spirits of Spices
Distill with a gentle heat either in balneo or ashes the strong and sweete water where with you haue drawen oils of cloues, mace, nutmegs, Iuniper, Rosemarie, &c. after it hath stoode one moneth close stopt, and so you shall purchase most delicate spirit of each of the saide aromaticalle bodies.[132]

Distilling the spirit with essential oils instead of fresh or dried materials meant the intensity of the botanicals' aromas and flavours were diminished after resting in a closed container for a month. This is why the resulting spirit was unusually subtle for the period.

Plat's three spirits recipes would have been accomplished in a cold still. However, better qual-

---

131.   Hugh Plat, *Delightes for Ladies, to Adorne Their Persons, Tables, Closets, and Distillatories* (London: Peter Short, 1602), b3.

132.   Hugh Plat, *Delightes for Ladies, to Adorne Their Persons, Tables, Closets, and Distillatories* (London: Peter Short, 1602), b3.

ity and greater quantity could have been produced in a hot still— more familiarly called a pot still.[133] A rounded head was secured to the still's body that accommodated additional air circulation and vapour concentration. Filled with infused liquid, the hot still was set over a brick furnace fitted with an aperture that allowed the still to rest either over indirect heat or in a balneo marie. The still's head and its swan-like neck allowed the capture of escaped steam, sending it down the length of the neck by natural gravity and air pressure to the worm—a serpentine tube—nestled into a cooling tub filled with cold water. Thus, the alcohol vapours condensed against the cold sides of the worm and flowed out the other end into a receiving vessel. While copper became the preferred metal for the still's body, recent studies suggest that pewter was employed to fashion the worm and the swan's neck for economic reasons.[134]

---

133.   Constance Anne Wilson, *Water of Life: A History of Wine-Distilling and Spirits 500 BC to AD 2000* (Totnes, Devon: Prospect Books, 2006), 197.

134.   Trish Hayward and Peter Hayward, 'Pewter Stills', in *Journal of the Pewter Society*, Autumn 2013, 5.

(Although the dangers of lead poisoning had been recognised and documented as early as 2000 BC, it did not seem of particular concern in Britain or the American colonies until the mid-eighteenth century. One of the newly-formed United States' first public health laws banned the use of lead in condensing coils.[135])

Smaller quantities of spirits were also effectively distilled in an enhanced version of an earlier stillatory called a Moorshead still.[136] A revised design called the bucket-head still had its main components fashioned out of copper.[137] A highly reactive metal, copper binds with the sulphur compounds found in wine and beer, removing impurities plus offensive aromas and flavours in the resulting spirit. Pewter versions were manufactured and sold at a cheaper price. However,

---

135.   Herbert L. Needleman, 'History of Lead Poisoning in the World', Center for Biological Diversity < https://www.biological-diversity.org/campaigns/get_the_lead_out/pdfs/health/Needleman_1999.pdf> [accessed 21 February 2024].

136.   Constance Anne Wilson, *Water of Life: A History of Wine-Distilling and Spirits 500 BC to AD 2000* (Totnes, Devon: Prospect Books, 2006), 197-198.

137.   Trish Hayward and Peter Hayward, 'Pewter Stills', in *Journal of the Pewter Society*, Autumn 2013, 4.

pewter's lead and tin content did not produce the same magic when it encountered the spirit as copper did. But for some distillers, pewter stills made equipping a business venture more feasible. Either way, the bucket-head still made from either metal was heat-resistant, withstanding the temperature of a naked fire because the head or dome was surrounded by a large bucket of cold water or refrigeratory. Thus, the liquid inside heated rapidly and quickly concentrated vapours, which produced a higher alcohol-by-volume (ABV) content. Ascending from the still's body up the neck, the vapours further cooled while passing the still's head which was continuously cooled with water before streaming down the swan's neck to the receiving vessel. This allowed for the purer extraction of liquid essence, producing purer hydrosols or non-alcoholic waters.

Changes in the English economy as the country shifted from an agrarian base to a capitalistic one triggered a major transition in spirits production amongst many early modern English distillers who switched from wine spirits to grain

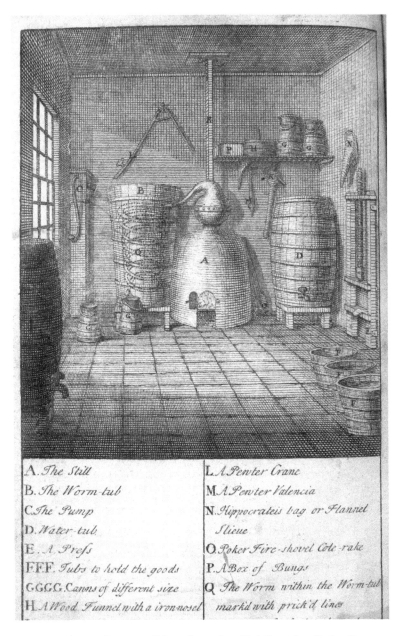

A. *The Still*	L. *A Pewter Crane*
B. *The Worm-tub*	M. *A Pewter Valencia*
C. *The Pump*	N. *Hippocrateis bag or Flannel*
D. *Water-tub*	*Sleeve*
E. *A Press*	O. *Poker Fire-shovel Cole-rake*
F.F.F. *Tubs to hold the goods*	P. *A Box of Bungs*
G.G.G.G. *Canns of different size*	Q *The Worm within the Worm-tub*
H. *A Wood Funnel with a iron-nosel*	*mark'd with prick'd lines*

A hot still or pot still from George Smith's A Compleat Body of Distillling (Source: private collection).

spirits. (Wine was an expensive import. Beer was made in nearly every English kitchen.) Profitability was of the greatest importance to producers as price was to consumers. Historian Tim Unwin suggested that differing taxation rates on wine imports changed consumption and production patterns, reflecting 'the various changing political alliances of the period.'[138] In other words, wine consumption by England's gentry was stymied by price hikes. The domestic and commercial distilling trades were also impacted as English distillers resorted to producing spirits from local beer or ale, or directly from fermented malted grain. This transition is seen in the 1615 edition of *Countrey Contentments or The English Huswife*. Written by Gervase Markham who, just like his contemporary Hugh Plat, was better known as a poet, horse breeder, and soldier of fortune than a distiller or brewer. However, Markham's domestic advice manual was his best-selling work. The recipe in his *English Huswife* for *aqua compositæ*—despite

---

138.   Tim Unwin, *Wine and Vine: An Historical Geography of Viticulture and the Wine Trade* (London: Routledge: 1991), 238.

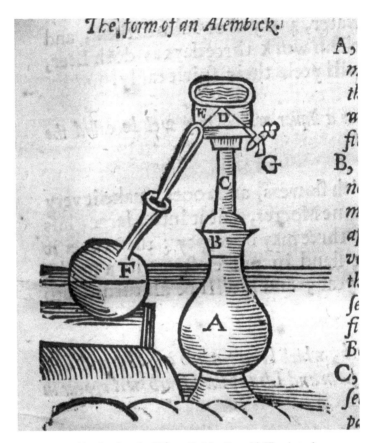

A bucket-head still from Dr John French's The Art of Distillation *(Source: private collection).*

Markham's lack of qualifications or authority on the subject—seems to have been acquired from a knowledgeable source who had actually produced a distillate by this means. [139]

> **To make aqua composita**
> Take rosemary, Time, Issop, Sage, fenell nip, roots of elicompane, of ech an handful, or marierum, and penyroall of ech half a handful; eight slippes of red mynt, halfe a pound of Licoras, halfe a pound of aniseeds and two gallons of the nest Ale that can be brewed, wash all the hearbes cleane, & put into the Ale, licoras, aniseeds, and hearbes into a cleane brasse pot, and set your limbecked thereon and paste it round about that no ayre come out then distill the water with a gentle fire, and kept the limbecked coole aboue, not suffering it to runne too fast and take heede when your water changeth collour, to put another glasse vnder, and keepe the first water, for it is most precious, and the latter

---

139. Gervase Markham, *Countrey Contentment, or The English Huswife* (London: R. Jackson, 1615), 131-132.

water keepe by itself, and put it into
you next pot, and that shall make it
much better.[140]

Make note that the use of the second
extraction spirit in this recipe as a base for rectifying the next round of *aqua compositæ* would in
turn intensify the flavour of the next batch. It was
a unique technique that only appeared a few more
times in distillation books.

Later in the century, *The Queen's Closet
Opened* was a book published in 1655, that was
reputedly authored by Walter Montagu who was
an English courtier, Bènèdictine abbot, and close
confidante to Charles I's Queen Henrietta Maria.
In his compendium, there is a formula for 'Clary
water for the Back, Stomach, Etc.' which demonstrated that beer was used instead of wine even
amongst the gentry who would not have changed
to beer for distillation for economic reasons, but
because there was a shift in taste preferences.[141]

---

140.   Gervase Markham, *Countrey Contentment, or The English
Huswife* (London: R. Jackson, 1615) 131-132.

141.   Walter Montagu, *The Queen's Closet Opened* (London: E Blagrave, 1696), 289.

Clary water for the Back, Stomach, &c.

Take three gallons of midling Beere, put it in a great brass pot of four gallons, and put to it ten handfuls of Clarey gathered in a dry day, Raysins of the Sun stoned three pounds, Aniseeds and Liquroice of each four unces, the whites and shels of twenty four Egges, or half so mayn if there be not so much need in the Back, the shels small and mixe them with the whites, put to the ottomes of three white loaves: put into the received one pound of white Sugarcandy, or so much fine loaf Sugar beaten small, and distill it through a Limback, keep it close, and be seldome without it for it reviveth very much the Stomach and Heart, strengheneth the Back, procureth appetite and digestion, driveth away melancholy, sadness and heaviness of the heart, &c. [142]

---

142.   Walter Montagu, *The Queen's Closet Opened* (London: E Blagrave, 1696), 289.

Another formula titled 'A Plague water to be taken one spoonful every four hours with one hours Sweat every Time' also called for distilling botanicals with strong beer.[143]

> **A Plague water to be taken one spoonful every four hours with one hours Sweat every Time**
> Take Scabious, Betony, Pimpernel, and Turmentine roots, of each a pound, steep these one night in three gallons of strong Beer, and distill them all in a Limback, and when you use it, take a spoonful thereof every four hours, and sweat well after it, draw two quarts of water, if your Beer be strong, and mingle them both together.[144]

As is seen in Montagu's recipes, the use of beer or malted grain as a base for distillation made inroads into domestic distillation just like it had amongst fifteenth-century German housewives. Cheaper and more readily available than imported

---

143.   Walter Montagu, *The Queen's Closet Opened* (London: E Blagrave, 1696), 243-244.

144.   Walter Montagu, *The Queen's Closet Opened* (London: E Blagrave, 1696), 243-244.

European wines, this close association between beer and spirits shaped the drinking tastes of seventeenth-century consumers.

Besides wine, ale, and beer, popular seventeenth-century advice manual authors such as physician Dr John French employed more questionable base liquids such as vitriol and turpentine. It was later claimed that much of his most famous work was nothing more than a translation of Hieronymous Brunschwig's work, which suggests that he adapted material from Laurens Andrewe's 1527 translation.[145] These base spirits can be seen paired with juniper berries and other botanicals in French's second edition of *The Art of Distillation or, a Treatise of the Choicest Spagiricall PREPARATIONS Performed by way of Distillation* which was published in 1653. One formula titled 'A Water against the Convulsions' was recommended for curing vertigo, the 'Hystericall Passion', epilepsy, 'all offenseive vapours and wind that annoys the head and stomach', as well as convulsions in

---

145.   Anonymous, 'Distillation', *Industrial Engineering Chemistry*, 28/6 (1936), 677.

children. Its base distillate was questionable—that being the 'dew of vitriol' or the 'humidity of the salt' that results from heating sulphur at a high temperature.[146]

A Water against the Convulsions

Take of Ros vitrioli (which is that water that is distilled from Vitriall in the calcining thereof) two quarts, in this put of Rue a handful, of Juniper berries bruised an ounce, of Bay berries bruised a half an ounce, Piony berries bruised six drams, Camphire two drams, Rhubarb sliced an ounce; digest these four days in a temperate Balneo, then distill them in a glass vessel in ashes,

---

146.   Dr. John French, *The art of distillation, or, A treatise of the choicest spagyrical preparations, experiments, and curiosities, performed by way of distillation : together with the description of the choicest furnaces and vessels used by ancient and modern chymists, and the anatomy of gold and silver ... in six books / by John French ... ; to which is added in this fourth impression Sublimation and calcination in two books ; as also The London-distiller* (London: E. Cotes for T.Williams, 1667), 50.

and there will come over a water of
no small virtue.[147]

Another remedy devised by Dr French
paired juniper berries with Venice turpentine as
a remedy for kidney stones:

An excellent water against the stone in the Kidneys

Take the middle rind of the root
of Ash bruised, two pound. Juniper berries bruised, three pound.
Venice turpentine that is very pure,
2 pound and a half. Put these into
twelve pints of spring water in a
glass vessel well closed, and there let
them putrifie in horse dung for the
space of three months, then distill
them in ashes, and there will come
forth an oil and a water, separate
from one another.
Ten or twelve drops of this oil being
taken every morning in four or six

---

147.   Dr. John French, *The art of distillation, or, A treatise of the
choicest spagyrical preparations, experiments, and curiosities, performed by way of distillation : together with the description of the choicest furnaces and vessels used by ancient and modern chymists, and
the anatomy of gold and silver ... in six books / by John French ... ; to
which is added in this fourth impression Sublimation and calcination in two books ; as also The London-distiller* (London: E. Cotes for
T.Williams, 1667), 50.

spoonfuls of the said water dissolves the gravell and stone in the kidneys, most wonderfully.[148]

Dr French further employed juniper berries in recipes for a distilled treacle vinegar that was administered to prevent infection and encourage sweating in those suffering from infection as well as a more complicated remedy for kidney stones that involved infusing and distilling more than two dozen botanicals.[149]

A distilled Treacle Vinegar.

Take of the roots of Bistort, Gentian, Angelica, Tormentill of each ten drams. Pimpernell, Bay berries, Juniper berries of each an ounce,

---

148.   Dr. John French, *The art of distillation, or, A treatise of the choicest spagyrical preparations, experiments, and curiosities, performed by way of distillation : together with the description of the choicest furnaces and vessels used by ancient and modern chymists, and the anatomy of gold and silver … in six books / by John French … ; to which is added in this fourth impression Sublimation and calcination in two books ; as also The London-distiller* (London: E. Cotes for T.Williams, 1667), 54-55.

149.   Dr. John French, *The art of distillation, or, A treatise of the choicest spagyrical preparations, experiments, and curiosities, performed by way of distillation : together with the description of the choicest furnaces and vessels used by ancient and modern chymists, and the anatomy of gold and silver … in six books / by John French … ; to which is added in this fourth impression Sublimation and calcination in two books ; as also The London-distiller* (London: E. Cotes for T.Williams, 1667), 54-55.

Nutmeg, five drams, The shavings of Sassafras, two ounces, Zedoary half a dram, White Sanders, three drams, The leves of Rue, Wormwood, Scordium of each half a handful, The flowers of Wall-flower, Buglosse of each a handful and half, Andromachus Treacle, Mithridate of each six drams, Infuse them all in three pints of the best White wine vinegar the space of eight days in *Frigido* [in coldness] in glass vessels; then distill in Balneo.[150]

Another water for the same use.
Take the juice of Radish, Lemmons, of each a pound and half: Waters of Betony, Tansey, Saxifrage, and Vervin, of each a pint. Hydromell, and Malmsey, of each two pound. In this Liquors mixed together, infuse fot the space of four or five days in

150.   Dr. John French, *The art of distillation, or, A treatise of the choicest spagyrical preparations, experiments, and curiosities, performed by way of distillation : together with the description of the choicest furnaces and vessels used by ancient and modern chymists, and the anatomy of gold and silver ... in six books / by John French ... ; to which is added in this fourth impression Sublimation and calcination in two books ; as also The London-distiller* (London: E. Cotes for T.Williams, 1667), 54.

a gentle Balneo, Juniper berries ripe and newly gathered being bruised, three ounces: the seed of Gromel, Bur-dock, Radish, Saxifrage, Nettles, Onions, Anise, and fennell, of each an ounce and half, the four cold seeds, the seed of great Mallows, of each six drams, the Calx of Eg-shels, Cinnamon, of each three drams, of Camphire two drams, let all be well strained and distilled in ashes.[151]

Whether you want to believe the credibility or efficacy of some of these early distillation recipes or not, one thing is certain. These books, these recipes, this all-consuming interest in spirits had taken hold of the English drinking culture, making it a new rival for the attentions of an eager and appreciative audience of English drinkers.

---

151.   Dr. John French, *The art of distillation, or, A treatise of the choicest spagyrical preparations, experiments, and curiosities, performed by way of distillation : together with the description of the choicest furnaces and vessels used by ancient and modern chymists, and the anatomy of gold and silver ... in six books / by John French ... ; to which is added in this fourth impression Sublimation and calcination in two books ; as also The London-distiller* (London: E. Cotes for T.Williams, 1667), 54-55.

CHAPTER FOUR

'...DRAWING DOUBLE THE QUANTITY OF AQUA VITÆ...'[152]

Conspicuous consumption took distillation out of the house and into the streets. That's when London's distillers got organised and gave us the first look at a London-style juniper distillate recipes.

AT THIS POINT, we need to take a moment to consider how these seventeenth-century distillates spread beyond London's apothecary shops and household distilleries into more commercial environs. Although England's consumer revolution is gen-

---

152.   Great Britain, *Titles of Patents of Invention Chronologically arranged From March 2, 1617 (14 James I.) to October 1, 1852 (16 Victoriæ): Part I, Nos. 1 to 4,800, pages 1 to 784,* ed. by Bennett Woodcroft (London: HMSO, 1854), 17.

erally associated with the eighteenth century, historian Jon Stobart noted that there are examples of 'a close relationship between the advent of new goods and new modes of selling in the previous century.'[153] Retailing was a novel approach to selling goods as consumers shifted their attention away from domestically produced items. Stobart commented that 'The so-called "shopping galleries"', which were founded in seventeenth-century London's commercial exchanges were each associated with specific goods, sales techniques, and audiences.[154] The Royal Exchange, built in 1567, was London's first commercial and financial exchange. It offered retailers rented stalls in which they could trade their wares in a business and social atmosphere.[155] Heading westward from

---

153.   Jon Stobart, 'A history of shopping: the missing link between retail and consumer revolutions', *Journal of Historical Research in Marketing*, 2/3 (2010)t, 343.

154.   Jon Stobart, 'A history of shopping: the missing link between retail and consumer revolutions', *Journal of Historical Research in Marketing*, 2/3 (2010), 343.

155.   Vicki Howard and Jon Stobart, 'Arcades, shopping centres, and shopping malls', *The Routledge Companion to the History of Retailing*, ed. by Jon Stobart and Vicki Howard (London: Routledge, 2018), 197.

Cornhill, in 1609, Westminster Hall had outlets that appealed to gentlemen shoppers while the New Exchange offered aristocratic ladies a place to shop and socialise. In both scenarios, conspicuous consumption (aka: consumerism) took a firm grasp on the English psyche and pocketbook. What did this mean for the seventeenth-century distilling trade? Returning to Plat's 1602 book *Delightes for Ladies,* one chapter was titled 'How to make the ordinarie Spirit of wine, that is solde for 5 shillings, & a noble [about £126 today], a pinte' suggested that spirits were a new and potentially profitable commodity.[156]

> **2. How to make the ordinary Spirit of wine that is sold for five shillings and a nobble a pinte.**
> Put Sacke, Malmesie, or a Muskadine into a glasse boady, leaving one third or more of your glasse empty, set it in balneo, or in a pan of ashes, keeping a soft and gentle fire: draw no longer thana till all or most part will burne away, which you ma prove

---

156.   Hugh Plat, *Delightes for Ladies, to Adorne Their Persons, Tables, Closets, and Distillatories* (London: Peter Short, 1602, b2.

now and then, by setting a spoone-
ful thereof on fire with a paper, as
it droppeth from the nose or pipe
of the helme: & if your spirit thus
drawn have any phlegme therein,
then rectifie or re-distill that spirit
again in a lesser body, or in a bolt
reciever instead of another body,
luting a small head on the top of the
steele thereof, and so you shall have
a very strong spirit: or else for more
expeidition, distill 5. Or 6. Gallons
of wine by Limbecke; and that spirit
which ascendeth afterward, re-distill
in glasses, as before.

Distillers' shops and 'hot water houses'—
the cousins of the traditional ale houses—popped
up to service the city's thirsty drinking culture,
offering a new cultural framework in which con-
viviality could be nurtured.[157] (Hot water houses.
Puritan politician William Prynne denounced
spirits drinking in his 1663 play *Histrio-mastrix*:
The Player's Scourage or Actor's Tragedy, in which

---

157.   Constance Anne Wilson, *Water of Life: A History of Wine-
Distilling and Spirits 500 BC to AD 2000* (Totnes, Devon: Prospect
Books, 2006), 213.

he called consumers of spirits 'hot-water-house haunters.'[158]) At this point, anyone in seventeenth-century England who could afford to purchase a still of any design, measuring tools, storage equipment, a printed advice manual, and to rent a space in which to operate in a commercial district could set up a distiller's shop. And indeed, many did. Historian R.J. Forbes noted that in early modern London 'it took £2,000 to £10,000 [about £275,750 and £1,378,770 today] to build a brewery whilst a distillery required only £500 to £5,000 [about £68,938 and £689,384 today]' in capital investment.[159] Unlike the physical plant and space needed for commercial brewing that included at least a few mash vats, brewing kettles, guile vats, coolers, and storage barrels, and a strong, able-bodied workforce, distilleries needed only a modicum of equipment, space, and a much smaller workforce. Fitted with a single pot still or sev-

---

158.   William Prynne, *Histrio-mastrix: The Player's Scourage or Actor's Tragedy* (London: Printed by E.A. and W.I. for M. Sparke, 1633), 21.

159.   R. J. Forbes, *Short History of the Art of Distillation: From the Beginnings up to the Death of Cellier Blumenthal* (Leiden: Brill, 1948), 195.

eral pot stills plus a few containers for storage, an aspiring distiller could set up shop and profit from the hottest new drink trend in seventeenth-century London. The need to regulate early modern English housewives, apothecary shops, and distiller's shops who comprised this emerging trade in distilling spirits became obvious as consumer habits ramped up in favour of recreational spirits consumption.

That's enough about conspicuous consumption for now. Let's get back to the topic of gin. The distinction as we now know between genever and modern-day gin had its origins in the seventeenth-century English distilling trade's professionalisation. The catalyst in this upward mobility of the trade in London was Théodore Turquet de Mayerne. The Swiss-born son of French historian Louis Turquet de Mayerne, Théodore studied at the Montpellier School of Medicine in France whose faculty included the twelfth-century Catalan alchemist and physician Arnaud de Villeneuve (who was the first European to distil alcohol from wine) and the thirteenth-century

Catalan mystic Ramon Llull (who first scientifically analysed the effect of multiple distillations on a single spirits batch.)[160] De Mayerne had a strong academic pedigree when it came to distilling spirits. De Mayerne served as physician-in-ordinary to King Henri IV of France until in 1610, when the monarch was assassinated. The next year de Mayerne was appointed to the position of the primary physician to King James I of England and his queen, Anne of Denmark. (Remember her? She imported the Danish spirits drinking culture to the English royal court.) Elected in 1616 as a Fellow of the Royal College of Physicians, de Mayerne's interest in iatrochemistry and the Crown's obvious appreciation for social spirits consumption, played a significant role in professionalising the seventeenth-century English distilling trade.

The first step toward legitimising distillation took place amongst the city's apothecaries.

---

160.   R. J. Forbes, *Short History of the Art of Distillation: From the Beginnings up to the Death of Cellier Blumenthal* (Leiden: Brill, 1948), 60; Hugh Redwald Trevor-Roper, *Europe's physician: the various life of Sir Theodore de Mayerne* (London: Yale University Press, 2006), 44-46; Michael Berlin, *The Worshipful Company of Distillers: A Short History* (Chichester: Phillimore & Co. Ltd., 1996), 7 and 10.

It started when James I granted Gideon de Laune (who was Queen Anne of Denmark's apothecary) a monopoly, in 1617, to establish the Worshipful Society of Apothecaries. The Society's role was to ensure London's apothecaries were the sole providers and purveyors of medicines—distilling, compounding, and dispensing preparations the College's physicians prescribed. In other words, female distillers were cut out of the equation—at least within London city limits. De Mayerne worked with the College to publish the Society's manual, *Pharmacopoeia Londinensis,* in 1618, which standardised the recipes for both distillates and compounded medicines that were manufactured by its members . In this manual, listed under '*Aqvæ Simplico*' or 'simple waters', there was an *Aqua Juniperi ex granis*.[161] But because there was no accompanying recipe, it is possible to assume that it was made by distilling a pound of juniper berries with a gallon of 'proof spirit' and enough water to prevent empyreuma—or the burnt smell

---

161.   Royal College of Physicians, *Pharmacopoea Londinensis* (London: Edward Griffin, 1618), 18.

imparted by charred vegetable matter—when it was heated as was mentioned in a 1746 revised edition of this standards manual.[162]

While the Society oversaw medicine making throughout London, a growing demand for distilled spirits in popular drinking culture—amongst the new droves of conspicuous consumers—created a new revenue stream for a swelling number of commercial distillers. Naturally, this triggered a surging outcry for regulation. Before distiller's shops produced *aqua vitæ* and *aqua compositæ* as social spirits, London's commercial distilleries made a good profit from distilling vinegar from surplus ale and beer that was purchased from the city's breweries.[163] Why vinegar? Sixteenth-century chronicler and antiquarian John Strype noted 'That in the beginning of the Wars in the Low Countries [the Eighty Years' War (1566-1648)],

162. Royal College of Physicians of London, *The new dispensatory of the Royal College College of Physicians in London. With copious and accurate indexes. Faithfully translated from the Latin of the Pharmacopoia Londinensis, publish'd by order of the King and Council* (London: printed for the translator, and sold by W. Owen), 1746.

163. Company of Distillers of London, *The Distiller of London*, ed. by Anistatia R. Miller and Jared M. Brown (London: Mixellany Limited, 2020), 61-62.

the Flemings bought great Quantities of this kind of Beeregre [a vinegar distilled from beer] for the cooling of their Ordinance, and was sold at good Prices to the Spaniards...'[164] But the popular drinking culture contributed to shifting this business model, making rectified spirits such as geneva the London distillers' best-selling commodity. As eighteenth-century distiller Ambrose Cooper recounted: 'There was formerly kept in the Apothecaries Shops a stilled spirituous Water of Juniper, but the Vulgar being fond of it as a Dram, the Distillers supplanted the Apothecaries, and sold it under the Name of Geneva.'[165] His statement and the item listed in the *Pharmacopoeia Londinensis* suggest that there was a difference between the apothecary's Water of Juniper or *Aqua Juniperi ex granis* and the commercial distillers' geneva.

So, what was geneva? The answer depends a lot on whether you are talking about making

---

164.   John Strype, 'GLOVERS, TINNERS, DISTILLERS,' in *The Survey of the Cities of London and Westminster, Book 5* (London: 1598, reprinted J.M. Dent & Sons, Ltd., 1720), 236-237.

165.   Ambrose Cooper, *The Complete Distiller* (London: P. Vaillant, 1757), 248.

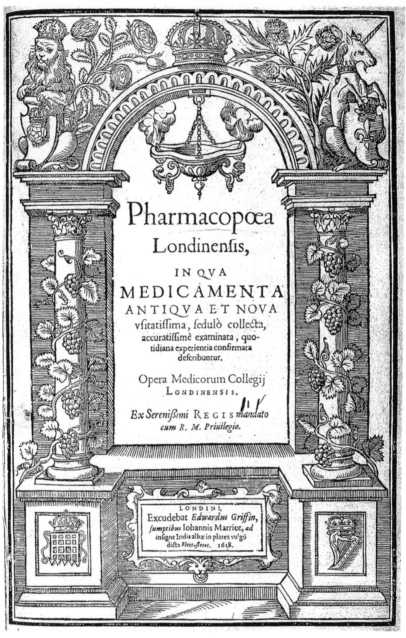

Pharmacopœa
Londinensis,

IN QVA
MEDICAMENTA
ANTIQVA ET NOVA
vſitatiſsima, ſedulò collecta,
accuratiſsimè examinata, quo-
tidiana experientia confirmata
deſcribuntur.

Opera Medicorum Collegij
LONDINENSIS.

Ex Sereniſsimi REGIS *mandato
cum R. M. Priuilegio.*

LONDINI,
Excudebat *Edwardus Griffin,*
ſumptibus Iohannis Marriot, *ad
inſigne Iridis albæ* in platea vu'gò
dicta *Fleet-ſtreet.* 1618.

Opening page of the 1618 edition of Pharmacopoea
Londinensis.

Dutch geneva or English geneva. Eighteenth-century physician Peter Shaw described the production for both spirits during the seventeenth and eighteenth centuries, observing that in Holland:

> ...the **Malt-Stiller** gives his Spirit a single Rectification *per se*, in order to purify it a little, and make it up *proof*,...or to be distilled with **Juniper Berries** or other Ingredients, into Geneva, or other Compound Waters for the vulgar. And this is all the Rectification the **Malt-Spirit** made in **Holland** usually undergoes: the Method there, being able to distil their Low-Wines to full **Proof-Spirit;** and then directly make it into **Geneva...** [166]

In other words, Shaw perceived that the major point of difference between Dutch geneva and English geneva was that Dutch distillers had 'little notion' of 'Rectification; and [the] making of double Spirit.' [167] (Rectification is the term used

166.   Peter Shaw, *Three Essays in Artificial Philosophy or Universal Chemistry* (London: J. Osborn and T. Longman, 1731), 114-115.

167.   Peter Shaw, *Three Essays in Artificial Philosophy or Universal Chemistry* (London: J. Osborn and T. Longman, 1731), 114-115.

to describe the process of purifying and intensifying a spirit through repeated distillations, producing a purer essence and increasing the liquid's alcohol content.) Consequently, Shaw opined that Dutch distillers 'leave their common Spirit so foul, and coarse as renders even the Geneva made with it very disagreeable,' adding that the offensive flavour is heightened substantially by 'their immoderate use of *Rye Meal*, in the production of their Spirit.'[168] In his analysis, Shaw pointed out two crucial differences. First, the Dutch distilled their low-wines—or the initial low-alcohol distillations—from a ferment made almost exclusively of rye meal and water. Second, the English distilled their low-wines with beer or fermented malted barley—free from rye meal—using repeated rectifications until the desired purity and higher alcohol content were achieved. This made Dutch geneva and English geneva as different in composition and manufacture as the differences between today's bourbon whiskey and scotch whisky.

---

168.   Peter Shaw, *Three Essays in Artificial Philosophy or Universal Chemistry* (London: J. Osborn and T. Longman, 1731), 114-115.

As the seventeenth century progressed, the trend toward the social consumption of spirits exploded. Economic and social historian Joan Thirsk determined that by 1621 residents of London and Westminster were serviced by no less than 200 distiller's shops.[169] But according to historian John Burnett there were also rogue distillers selling 'British brandy' that was reportedly manufactured from beer dregs, wine lees, rotten fruit, and other undesirable but fermentable material.[170] In their ground-breaking 1957 book *The Englishman's Food: Five Centuries of English Diet*, historians J.C. Drummond and Anne Wilbreham defined 'British brandy' as spirits distilled from 'raw materials other than wine.'[171] However, since many distillers—both domestic and commercial—found beer and ale more suitable ferments for distillation

---

169.   Joan Thirsk, *Economic Policy and Projects: The Development of a Consumer Society in Early Modern England* (Oxford: Clarendon Press, 1978; reprinted 1988), 97.

170.   John Burnett, *Liquid Pleasures: A Social History of Drink in Modern Britain* (London: Routledge, 1999), 161; John Watney, *Mother's Ruin: A History of Gin* (London: Peter Owen, 1976), 161.

171.   J.C. Drummond and Anne Wilbreham, *The Englishman's Food: Five Centuries of English Diet* (London: Jonathan Cape, 1939, revised 1957), 116.

and rectification as seen in the advice manuals of the day. This 'British brandy' was more than likely distilled from the less-desirable items mentioned earlier by John Burnett.

A group of outraged commercial distillers petitioned the House of Commons, on 27 February 1621, to pass legislation to outlaw London's rogue distillers. Titled *An Act for Relieving of the Distillers and Sellers of Aqua Vita, Aqua Compostia, and other strong and hot waters, in London and Westmynstere, and the Liberties and Suburbs thereof, and within seven miles compass of the same*, the bill fell on deaf ears.[172] Consequently, Parliament accomplished little that year to stem the tide of bad liquor production.

Then, *An Act concerning Monopolies and Dispensations with penall laws and the Forfeyture thereof* was passed by Parliament on 12 February 1624.[173] It was a significant step toward regulating the activities of trades in England, including distilling. The

---

172.   Great Britain, 'House of Commons Journal Volume I 27 February 1621,' *Journal of the House of Commons, Volume I, 1547-1629* (London, 1802), 529-531; Drummond and Wilbreham, 115.

173.   21 James I, c.3.

statute opened the doors for de Mayerne and physician Thomas Cademan to apply for and receive Patent #81, on 25 March 1635, which allowed them to distil spirits and make vinegars from 'cider, perry, and bucke or French wheate, where of they have byn the inventors' for a yearly rent of £10 (about £1,200 today), which was payable to King Charles I for a period of 14 years.[174] Sadly, there are no records of the actual process that de Mayerne and Cademan proposed to employ.[175] The next year, Cademan and another of his associates, Sir William Brouncker, who was a gentleman of the Privy Chamber, received Patent #90 on 26 March 1636 for 'Drawing double the quantity of aqua-vitæ from a given quantity of liquor; also extracting a larger quantity of strong water from

---

174.   Great Britain, *Titles of Patents of Invention Chronologically arranged From March 2, 1617 (14 Janes I.) to October 1, 1852 (16 Victoriæ): Part I, Nos. 1 to 4,800, pages 1 to 784*, ed. by Bennett Woodcroft (London: HMSO, 1854), 17; Michael Berlin, *The Worshipful Company of Distillers: A Short History* (Chichester: Phillimore & Co. Ltd., 1996), 10; Frederic Arthur Filby, *A History of Food Adulteration and Analysis* (London: G. Allen & Unwin Limited, 1934), 157.

175.   Frederic Arthur Filby, *A History of Food Adulteration and Analysis* (London: G. Allen & Unwin Limited, 1934), 157.

malt than has hitherto been usual.'[176] This patent suggests that Cademan and Brouncker manufactured sizeable quantities of neutral grain spirit from fermented malt (Read: Distilling spirit from beer or ale.) The two men set up production in 'a house described as on the backside of St. James' Park', which by some accounts was situated across the road from St James's Palace on Cleveland Road near Brouncker's home on St James's Street.[177] (Their enterprise was such a success that in 1633, Brouncker and Cademan petitioned to relocate their operations 'being doubtful it might offend his Majesty's house if it were enlarged, which they have the necessity to do' and wished for the monarch to inspect their new distillery.[178])

176.   Great Britain, *Titles of Patents of Invention Chronologically arranged From March 2, 1617 (14 James I.) to October 1, 1852 (16 Victoriæ): Part I, Nos. 1 to 4,800, pages 1 to 784*, ed. by Bennett Woodcroft (London: HMSO, 1854), 17; Michael Berlin, *The Worshipful Company of Distillers: A Short History* (Chichester: Phillimore & Co. Ltd., 1996), 10.

177.   Michael Berlin, *The Worshipful Company of Distillers: A Short History* (Chichester: Phillimore & Co. Ltd., 1996), 10.

178.   Great Britain, *Calendar of State Papers, Domestic Series of the reign of Charles I. 1633-1634, Volume 6* (London: HMSO, 1863), 382.

Concerned for the reputations of both London's apothecaries and distillers—as well as his own and his colleagues' respective business interests—de Mayerne stepped up a campaign for the regulation of the distilling trade by publicly condemning the rising denigration by this:

> ...current of the disorderly and inordinate intrusion of Interlopers into the practice of this Art: who by their preposterous wayes of working, and frequent use of base and unsound materials, have brought scandall, not onely upon the works of this Art, (the wares) but also on the Art, and Artists themselves.[179]

To preserve the credibility of the city's commercial distilling trade, De Mayerne, Brouncker, and Cademan (who by 1626 was appointed physician-in-ordinary to Queen Henrietta Maria) along with 99 producers of 'spirits, *aqua vitæ*, strong waters, vinegars, and beeragers' obtained a monopoly, on 9 August 1638, establish-

---

179. Company of Distillers of London, *The Distiller of London*, ed. by Anistatia R. Miller and Jared M. Brown (London: Mixellany Limited, 2020), 6-7.

ing the Worshipful Company of Distillers.[180] This Company was established to monitor and regulate commercial distilleries in London, Westminster, and the surrounding 21-mile radius.[181] Just as he had accomplished to support London's apothecaries, de Mayerne edited and published a standards manual for the new guild in collaboration with Cademan. The 1639 *The Distiller of London* contained the Company's rules of conduct plus recipes for 34 approved 'strong waters' and 16 variations which were written in code to protect their 'mysteries' in both large and small quantities.[182] (The book later helped the Company to publicly lay claim to control of distilling trade when it was reprinted in 1669, 1698, and 1726.[183])

180.   Michael Berlin, *The Worshipful Company of Distillers: A Short History* (Chichester: Phillimore & Co. Ltd., 1996), 12.

181.   Company of Distillers of London, *The Distiller of London*, ed. by Anistatia R. Miller and Jared M. Brown (London: Mixellany Limited, 2020), 14.

182.   Company of Distillers of London, *The Distiller of London*, ed. by Anistatia R. Miller and Jared M. Brown (London: Mixellany Limited, 2020), passim.

183.   Michael Berlin, *The Worshipful Company of Distillers: A Short History* (Chichester: Phillimore & Co. Ltd., 1996), 15.

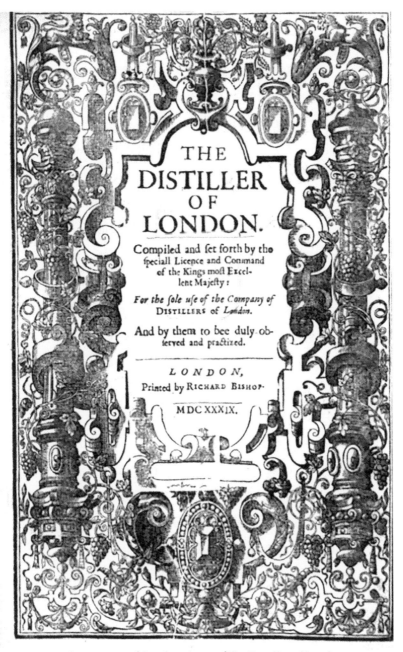

Opening page of the 1639 edition of The Distiller of London
(Source: private collection).

Thus, *The Distiller of London* provides insights into three significant changes in early modern English distillation. First, the average early modern English person had developed a sweet tooth—not just in food, but in beverages as well. All of the manual's recipes—called 'rules'— are spirits that are dulcified or sweetened with sugar or honey after rectification. These formulations not only demonstrate sugar's growing popularity in England, they also suggest the reason why these spirits were later popularly called 'sweets' in *An Act for repealing the present duty on Sweets,* which was passed on 21 June 1737.[184] Sweets were also the subject of *An act to amend Two Acts passed in the forty-fifth year of his present Majesty*, which was passed on 10 July 1817, ordering distillers to obtain separate licensing to 'brew or make for Sale any Liquor called Sweets or Made Wines'.[185] In other words, by the early nineteenth century, distillers who commercially produced the Com-

---

184.   10 George II, c.17.

185.   52 George III c.87.

pany's 'rules' from the manual needed a separate licence to produce their specialty spirits.

The second change seen in the manual's regulations narrated how rogue distillers produced spirits of a perceived lesser quality. One directive banned the Company's member-distillers from producing spirit from stale beer, stale ale, or brewers' afterwort which was nicknamed 'Blew-John'— a partially fermented remnant wash from the brewing process.[186] The Company also prohibited its member-distillers from using lees of wine, 'unwholesome Sugarwaters', or rotten fruit in their rectification. The manual further provided two standardised recipes for making vinegar.[187] However, the manual offered no instructions for distilling the 'strong-proofe' grain spirits employed in the Company's rules. It is unknown if this was an intentional omission because two of the Company's founders—Cademan

---

186. Company of Distillers of London, *The Distiller of London*, ed. by Anistatia R. Miller and Jared M. Brown (London: Mixellany Limited, 2020), 15.

187. Company of Distillers of London, *The Distiller of London*, ed. by Anistatia R. Miller and Jared M. Brown (London: Mixellany Limited, 2020), 16-17 and 59-62.

The Characters expreſsing the quantities, qualities, and kinds of Materials and Ingredients uſed in this Worke.

℞	Take	℥	Ounce
Q.S.	Sufficient quantity.	℔	Pound, or 16 ounces
ana	of Each.	☉	Reed roſes
S.A.	According to art	♃	Cloue gilliflouers.
B.M.	Hott Bath	△	Reed Poppie.
M.	Handfull	♂	Reed Saunders
□	Barrell	♃	Rape
Qr.	Quarter	♀	Mault
gr.	Graine	*	Hopps.
ʒ	Dram or ⅛ ounce.	A	Allum.

The ten ſmall Italica Letters (of the Alphabet)
below, are in all reſpects to be eſteem'd and valued, in whole numbers and fractions; as the numerall figures and cipher in Arithmetick, are:

As in Example.

1. 2. 3. 4. 5. 6. 7. 8. 9. 0.
y n v o c a t e r s

y y y v &c.
o v n o

The legend page for deciphering the recipes in 1639 edition of
The Distiller of London *was handwritten into each copy
given to member(Source: private collection).*

Bruife the pils and feeds.
Diftill them into ftrong proofe fpi-
rit, *S. A.*
Dulcifie with white fugar, × *c.*   ℞ ℥.

dbdbdbdbdbdb   dbb

X.

℞ Strong proofe fpirit, *Q. S.*   ℥ ℥.
Speire Mint,   ⎫
Lovage roots,   ⎬ dry,
Anifefeeds, *ana*, × *y.*   ℞ *y.* ℥ *c.*
Calamus Aromaticus,
Ginger,
Sweet Fennell feeds,
Imperatoria roots,
Wormwood dry, ftript,
            ana, ℥ *s*.   ℥ *t.*
Caruway   ⎱ feeds, *ana*, ℞ *a.*   ℥ *c.*
Coriander ⎰
Cumyne feeds,
Cloves, *ana*, ℞ *v.*   ℥ *n* ℥
Bruife them that are to bee
    bruifed.
Diftill them into ftrong proofe fpi-
rit, *S. A.*
Dulcifie with white fugar, × *c.*   ℞ ℥.
            H   XI.

The recipe for Rule X as it appeared in the 1639 edition of The
Disitller of London *(Source: private collection).*

and Brouncker— held patents in London on producing neutral grain spirits from malted grain or it was the authors' innocent oversight. A point for future research by historians could determine if the strong-proofe spirits mentioned in the manual's recipes were, in fact, produced in quantity by Cademan and Brouncker who held the patents on these goods and who then sold them to members.

The third and most important change to witness in *The Distiller of London* are three rules that featured juniper berries as a predominant botanical. The first recipe—Rule XXVI—for making *aqua ad crapulum* or Surfeit Water called for the rectification of 80 pounds of 'strong-proofe' or multi-distilled spirit with 16 botanicals:[188]

XXVI.
Take Strong proofe spirit, sufficient quantity.
Iuniper berries, 2 lb.
Enulacampana roots, dry, 1 lb.
Calamus aromatica,} of each, 4 oz.
Gallingall,} [ditto]

---

188.   Company of Distillers of London, *The Distiller of London*, ed. by Anistatia R. Miller and Jared M. Brown (London: Mixellany Limited, 2020), 37.

Wormwood, of each all dry,}
2-1/2 oz.

Speire Mint,} [ditto]

Red Mint,} [ditto]

Caruway seeds,} of each, 2 oz.

Angellica seeds,} [ditto]

Sassafras roots, with the bark,} of
each, 3 oz.

White Cynnamon,} [ditto]

Nuttmegs,} of each, 1 oz.

Maces,} [ditto] [189]

The final distillate was then dulcified with sugar.

The second recipe—Rule XXXI—for *aqua rosa solis* or Rosa Solis proper, rectified 'strong proofe' spirit with botanicals, then aromatised the liquid with musk and ambergris before colouring it with a tincture of clove gilliflowers or red roses and finally dulcifying it with sugar. [190]

XXXI.

Take Strong proofe spirit, 80 lb.

Ros solis, gathered in due season

---

189.   Company of Distillers of London, *The Distiller of London*, ed. by Anistatia R. Miller and Jared M. Brown (London: Mixellany Limited, 2020), 79.

190.   Company of Distillers of London, *The Distiller of London*, ed. by Anistatia R. Miller and Jared M. Brown (London: Mixellany Limited, 2020), 86-87.

and cleane pickt, 4 lb.

Iuniper berries, 3 lb.

Sassafras roots, with the bark,} of
each, ¼ oz.

Caruway seeds,} [ditto]

Marigold flowers, 1 lb.

Aniseeds, 1-1/2 lb.

Bruise them that are to bee bruised.

Distill them into strong proofe spirit,
according to art.

Take hereof, 7 lb., add thereto, 1 lb.,
of Aqua Number, 23, [*Rule XXIII,
Aqua Prætiosa*] dulcified.

Licorice bruised, 1 lb.

Dulcifie it with white sugar, 10 lb.

If you add No rules contain this
ingredient of the aforesaid Water
[*Rule XXIII, Aqua Prætiosa*], then in
stead [sic] thereof

Take Musk, 1 dr.

Ambergreice, 3 dr.

Colour it with the tincture of Cloue
Gilliflowers or Reed roses, sufficient
quantity, according to art.[191]

191. Company of Distillers of London, *The Distiller of London*,
ed. by Anistatia R. Miller and Jared M. Brown (London: Mixellany
Limited, 2020), 86-87.

Finally, the third recipe—Rule XXXIII—for *aqua fructum* or Water of Fruits redistilled 'strong proofe' spirit with botanicals and infused the liquid with strawberries and raspberries for ten days before being filtered and dulcified with sugar.[192]

XXXIII.

Take Strong proofe spirit, 80 lb.

Iuniper berries, 4 lb.

Quince parings dry,} of each, 2 lb.

Pyppin parings dry,} [ditto]

Lymon pills dry,} of each, 1 lb.

Orenge pills dry,} [ditto]

Nuttmeg, 4 oz.

Anise seeds, 2 lbs.

Cloves, 2 oz.

Distill them into proofe spirit, according to art.

To the spirit, adde

Straweberries, bruised,} of each, 5 lb.

Rasspisses, bruised,} [ditto]

Stirre them well together, and after 10 days, it being cleere, may be drawne off.

Then dulcifie it with sirrup made as

---

192.   Company of Distillers of London, *The Distiller of London*, ed. by Anistatia R. Miller and Jared M. Brown (London: Mixellany Limited, 2020), 89-90.

hereafter is taught.
And so let it stand till it be cleere
and then draw it off, for use.[193]

These three recipes inspired intense personal curiosity on our part about seventeenth-century distillates that included juniper berries. Taking a page from the practices of experimental archaeologists, we managed with very limited time and access to essential distillation equipment to recreate Rule XXXIII after Anistatia decoded all the 'rules' in the 1639 edition of *The Distiller of London* which we published on behalf of the Worshipful Company of Distillers of London in 2020.[194] (Please note that these deciphered recipes deviate from those found in the 1652 supplement to Dr. John French's 1653 edition of *Art of Distillation*

---

193.   Company of Distillers of London, *The Distiller of London*, ed. by Anistatia R. Miller and Jared M. Brown (London: Mixellany Limited, 2020), 87-88.

194.   Company of Distillers of London, *The Distiller of London*, new edition, ed. by Anistatia Miller and Jared Brown (Chippenham: Mixellany Limited, 2020), passim.

that purported to decode the manual's rules.[195]) We also want to issue a caveat here taken from the recent medieval brewing experiments conducted by Susan Flavin and a team of researchers.[196] The early modern English distillation equipment, techniques and —most importantly—the grain and botanicals themselves differed markedly in the sixteenth and seventeenth centuries from what modern-day distillers use today. Consequently, there is no way to accurately replicate an organic liquid such as a seventeenth-century rectified spirit, which was produced on different types of still designs by the Company's many member-distillers, using a grain spirit made from undefined malted grain species and botanicals with indeterminate provenance. If you don't already know

---

195. Dr. John French, *The art of distillation, or, A treatise of the choicest spagyrical preparations, experiments, and curiosities, performed by way of distillation : together with the description of the choicest furnaces and vessels used by ancient and modern chymists, and the anatomy of gold and silver ... in six books / by John French ... ; to which is added in this fourth impression Sublimation and calcination in two books ; as also The London-distiller* (London: E. Cotes for T.Williams, 1667), 18-19.

196. Susan Flavin, Marc Meltonville, Charlie Taverner, Joshua Reid, Stephen Lawrence, Carlos Belloch-Mollina, and John Morrissey, 'Understanding Early Modern Beer: An Interdisciplinary Case-Study', *The Historical Journal*, 66 (2023), 521.

this, the organoleptic differences amongst Mediterranean, northern European, and British Isles juniper berries are really quite distinctive. The same can be said for the types of oranges, lemons, and other citrus that were grown and imported to England in those days. Nevertheless, we came as close as possible to rectifying the materials in the recipe in a copper pot still of a design similar to the large-scale, pot still designs found in early modern England. We combined an unmalted barley grain spirit and a neutral grain spirit to make the 'strong-proofe' spirit that was macerated with Mediterranean juniper berries, quince peel from our garden, pippin apple peel, lemon peel, orange peel, nutmeg, anise seeds, and whole cloves for 24 hours before we rectified it in the 300-litre copper pot still known as 'Prudence' at the Sipsmith Distillery in London. The redistilled spirit was placed in used oak barrels for ten days which we infused with dried strawberries and raspberries before filtering and bottling it. We didn't dulcify the finished liquid like the Company's member-distillers did so we could analyse this spirit against modern-day gins.

We taste-tested this liquid against three modern-day London dry gins—Beefeater, Tanqueray, and Sipsmith—along with a panel consisting of the master distillers of Beefeater, Sipsmith, Plymouth, and Thames Distilleries on 21 February 2021.[197] The consensus reached by this panel was that Rule XXXIII for *aqua fructum* is a very close ancestor of modern-day gins. It is the earliest published recipe to follow this structure, exhibiting a similar balance of juniper berries to both citrus and spice. (For reference, the botanical mixture rectified with spirit in Beefeater London Dry Gin contains juniper berries, angelica root, angelica seeds, coriander seeds, liquorice root, almonds, orris root, Seville orange peel, and lemon peel. Sipsmith London Dry Gin rectifies juniper berries, orange peel, lemon peel, coriander seeds, orris root, liquorice root, angelica root,

---

197.   We are eternally grateful to Beefeater master distiller Desmond Payne, Plymouth master distiller Sean Harrison, and Thames Distillers master distiller Charles Maxwell for taking the time during the COVID-19 pandemic to meet online to taste and share their findings via a Zoom meeting.

cinnamon bark, cassia bark, and almonds. Tanqueray London Dry Gin redistills juniper berries, coriander seeds, angelica root, and liquorice.) There is one other critical point to muse on about the recipes—rules—we have just presented: They were not invented in 1639. They were invented earlier, but we don't know when. *The Distiller of London* contains the formulas that were already in production amongst the Company's member-distillers. (Read: they were standardised for use in this book so members could achieve some coherent consensus of what the legitimate trade should produce.) But the point is that they were already being commercially produced. The actual dates of creation are unknown. So, the formulations leave a lot of room for a broad trajectory of future research by historians.

Even though the rising conspicuous consumption that stimulated the retailing of goods such as the 'rules' produced by the Company's member-distillers, the ordinances or by-laws of the Worshipful Company of Distillers—which were agreed to and filed on 1 July 1639—stipulated that the Company was against 'hawking about the streets', declaring that:

> …it is ordeyned that noo person
> or persons of this Company afore-
> said inhabiting within the limits of
> this Incorporation shall from here-
> forth carry, send, convey or cause
> to be carried, sent or conveyed in
> any maner of Wares whatsoever
> appertaining or belonging to the
> Trade of a Distiller into any Inns,
> hostels, Taverns, Alehouse, victualling
> house, or other house whatsoever
> or shall carry the same in any Street
> or lanes or any place whatsoever
> within the present aforesaid there
> to be sould or offered to sale in a
> hawking, or forestalling manner. But
> that every person of this said Com-
> pany to shift sett his Wares in open
> Shopp, Warehouse, or other Roome
> of his own or in a convenient stand-
> ing place in a Market upon payne to
> forfeit and pay to some of twenty
> shillings currant money of England

to the use of the Company for
every tyme they shall offend.[198]

While the current history books on gin tell us that
the 1736 and 1738 Gin Acts were responsible for
curtailing the sales of spirits by anyone other than
licenced retailers and distillers, this item in the
Company's 1639 ordinances suggests that London's regulated distillers agreed to ban the sales of
their wares outside of authorised premises a whole
century earlier. This one by-law set the Company's
member-distillers distinctly apart from the city's
rogue distillers and the street sellers who later
were the highlighted purveyors of spirits during
the so-called Gin Craze.

Although the Worshipful Company of Distillers was granted a monopoly by the Crown, the
Company itself met with intense opposition from
London's Worshipful Company of Apothecaries
who felt these commercial distillers encroached
on the rights of their syndication. Yet Charles I
sided with the distillers, threatening to use 'some
coercive way for despatch of the business, and by

198.   Parliamentary Archives: HL/PO/JO/10/5/274

that means vindicate his honour.'[199] However, the inception of the Civil War in 1642 and the king's execution in 1649 meant the issuance of the Company's charter was delayed and its fate was uncertain until March 1658 when the City of London finally enrolled the document.[200] The restoration of the monarchy and the accession of Charles II during the 1660s heralded the Company's revival.

It was then that women were first inducted as Company member-distillers such as Judith Robins, who in 1666 joined the Company after having 'used the art for 24 years and 3 years as a widow.'[201] Other female inductees were the widows of Company member-distillers who continued to ply their husband's trade. During this period, the Company continued to increase its membership; to heighten its authority as a political body when it was granted livery status in November 1671; and

---

199.   Michael Berlin, *The Worshipful Company of Distillers: A Short History* (Chichester: Phillimore & Co. Ltd., 1996), 18.

200.   Michael Berlin, *The Worshipful Company of Distillers: A Short History* (Chichester: Phillimore & Co. Ltd., 1996),18.

201.   Michael Berlin, *The Worshipful Company of Distillers: A Short History* (Chichester: Phillimore & Co. Ltd., 1996), 38.

to elevate its prominence when James II granted it a new charter in 1687. At this point, the Company's most notable duties were to inspect distillers' premises four times a year and to defend its member-distillers against the abuses at the hands of the farmers of the excise—the agents charged with the duty of accounting for and collecting excise on commodities, including spirits which was instigated by Parliament four decades earlier.

While historian Michael Berlin echoed nineteenth-century temperance leader Richard Valpy French's comment that the Distilling Act of 1690 allowed any person 'to set up a distillery on giving ten days' notice to the excise', the act stated something entirely different.[202] *An Act for encouraging the Distilling of Brandy and Spirits from Corne and for laying several duties on Low Wines of Spirits of the first Extraction* (aka: the Distilling Act of 1690) to which Valpy referred actually stated that:

> Provided always and bee it enacted
> and declared by the authorities

---

202.   Richard Valpy French, *Nineteen Centuries of Drink in England: A History* (London: National Temperance Publication Depot, 1884), 245.

aforesaid that it shall and may be lawful to or for any person or persons during the continuance of this Act to make draw or distill for Sale or to be retailed any Low Wines or Spirits from Drinke brewed from malted Corne onely paying the Duties and being subject to all Fines and Penalties as any other Distillers are any Law Charter or other to the contrary not withstanding.[203]

In other words, anyone who paid excise taxes on the spirits they produced could manufacture alcohol regardless of their affiliation with a guild or lack thereof, with or without giving the Office of Excise notification.

However, the rapid expansion of London's distilling trade made it increasingly difficult for the Company to maintain control. As Michael Berlin noted:

The Distillers' Company came to represent the wealthier malt distillers and rectifiers who either sold raw spirits to smaller, more numer-

---

203.   2 William & Mary, c.9.

ous compound distillers or sold their products through licenced premises.[204]

London during the 1730s, according to Berlin, boasted the presence of about 1,500 distillers. At least 100 of these distillers—about 7 per cent—had assets of more than £1,000 (about £117,790 today). But another 1,200 small distillers—80 per cent—had assets worth less than £100 (about £11,780 today).[205] Essentially, the Company managed the activities of about 7 per cent to potentially 20 per cent of the city's distilling trade. You could say this lack of Company control was the trigger that vaulted the so-called Gin Craze (1720-1751) a couple of furlongs' lead ahead of regulated spirits production and sales.

Who were these small distillers who made up the greater portion of London's trade? Since they didn't belong to the Company, the only place

204. Michael Berlin, *The Worshipful Company of Distillers: A Short History* (Chichester: Phillimore & Co. Ltd., 1996), 46.

205. Peter Clark, 'The "Mother Gin" Controversy in the Early Eighteenth Century', *Transactions of the Royal Historical Society,* 38 (1988), 64; Michael Berlin, *The Worshipful Company of Distillers: A Short History* (Chichester: Phillimore & Co. Ltd., 1996), 46.

we could find a record of them was if they committed or were involved in a crime. For this, we headed to the records of The Old Bailey—the Central Criminal Court of England and Wales—to find out where they worked and the types of people they encountered. Areas of the city that were mentioned in the court's records during the 1720s and 1730s included: Russell Street near Covent Garden, Mackett's Court in Piccadilly, Fore Street, Warder Street, the Highstreet in St Giles's, Charing Cross, Stratford Bow, Windmill Street, Haymarket, Duke Street, Holbourn Bridge, Breadstreet Hill, and Tothill Street in Westminster.[206] Less wealthy distillers encountered thefts by customers and employees. For example, William Green was a distiller in St Dunstan's Hill, which is halfway between London Bridge and the Tower of London. A spinster named Barthia Fisher called in at his shop, requesting 'strong Waters'. While they exchanged money, Fisher stole Green's coat off the

---

206.   Old Bailey Proceedings Online. <https://www.oldbaileyonline.org>[accessed: 18 December 2023].

staircase railing and stuffed it in her apron.[207] She was caught, tried on 5 December 1722, and sentenced to transportation. (Read: She was shipped to the colonies and sold off as a 'servant'.) On 14 January 1726, laundress Mary Jolly was prosecuted for stealing five aprons and two shirts from her employer, distiller Mr. Atkinson, whose distillery was in Whitechapel.[208] But then distillers were also indicted for theft and other felonies. Such was the case of distiller Thomas Bonnamy of Stratford Bow, who was tried on 6 December 1732 for breaking and entering the home of Thomas Williamson, stealing a few items of household goods plus 17 glass bottles.[209] Whether by association and by coincidence, this level of the distilling trade is what historians have focussed their sights on demonstrating to the world. Even though, they

---

207.   Old Bailey Proceedings Online, December 1722. Trial of Barthia Fisher (t17221205-3). <https://www.oldbaileyonline.org> [accessed: 18 December 2023].

208.   Old Bailey Proceedings Online, January 1726. Trial of Mary Jolly (t17260114-46). <https://www.oldbaileyonline.org> [accessed: 18 December 2023].

209.   Old Bailey Proceedings Online, December 1732. Trial of Thomas Bonnamy (t17321206-68) <https://www.oldbaileyonline. org> [accessed: 18 December 2023].

represented a physical majority at the time, they were not the sole traders of the eighteenth-century distilling business.

As you can see, the emergence of the conspicuous consumption of spirits led to a legitimate need for organisation and regulation of the new commercial distilling trade. The Company's manual—*The Distiller of London*—showed us that the nascence of a modern-day style of gin was confirmed by the 1630s although we do not know precisely when this formula was first produced by London's commercial distillers. While the Worshipful Company of Distillers managed to successfully oversee the activities of the city's wealthier, large-scale distillers, it became increasingly difficult for them to monitor the explosion of small distillers who set up operations after the Distilling Act of 1690 let anyone distil who was willing to pay the excise for the goods that were produced. But the Crown could not have cared less about altruistic values like manufacturing high-quality products by approved methods. The Crown needed money and needed it fast. Now, we need to take a step back to understand why the Crown needed money from the distilling trade and how they got it.

CHAPTER FIVE

'...FOR ENCOURAGING THE DISTILLING OF BRANDY AND SPIRITS FROM CORNE'[210]

Then we discover the excise tax acts that fed a nearly bankrupt Crown in the 1600s did not put an end to beer sales or boost gin sales. It just forced distillers to lower their standards to keep up with demand.

THERE'S AN ADAGE from Christopher Bullock's 1716 comedy play *The Cobbler of Preston* that makes an apropos intro to our next discussion: '...'tis impossible to be sure of anything but Death and Taxes'.[211] Let's go

---

210.   1 William & Mary, c.34.

211.   Christopher Bullock, *The Cobbler of Preston*, fifth edition (London: S. Bladon, 1767), 21.

back to the 1620s to get some context. The financial hell that beset the English Crown took shape when Charles I ascended the throne in 1625, and inherited his father James I's debt load. It placed the entire country 'in such straits for money as not to be spoken of.'[212] It had all started when the lavish lifestyle that marked Elizabeth I's reign at the close of the Tudor dynasty paved a gilt-covered path to the debt-ridden Stuart dynasty. The irresistible urge to maintain a monarchical presence festooned with pomp and splendour burdened the Crown's purse, shrivelling it to a point of near insolvency. The royal tendency toward extravagant displays portended a series of financial crises that afflicted England's economy for about two centuries. When Elizabeth I died in 1603, the Crown was saddled with arrears of £422,749 (about £58,000,000 today). That debt was comprised of the late queen's personal purchases plus ongoing military costs that the Crown incurred in Ireland and Flanders, before it broke away from

---

212.   Frederick Charles Dietz, *English Public Finance 1558-1641* (London: The Century Co., 1932), 225.

the southern portion of the Netherlands. Financial losses from internal sources compounded this debt load because of the 'tendency of old revenues to decay' such as rents on royal lands and unprofitable licences granted to various projects. (Remember the monopoly on *aqua vitæ* production Elizabeth I granted to Richard Drake that we told you about before? Yeah, the venture wasn't as profitable as you might think for its time.)[213] So when the equally profligate James I and his wife Queen Anne ascended the throne in 1603, England was in dire straits. Subsidies and the exchequer accounts could only pay off £355,886 (about £50,000,000 today), leaving a balance due of £66,863 (about £9,000,000 today).[214]

The most effective mechanism devised by Parliament to remedy the financial crisis took 40 years to accomplish: The nationalisation of taxes on England's most profitable commodities, including beer, ale, and spirits. Passed on 22 July

---

213.   Frederick Charles Dietz, *English Public Finance 1558-1641* (London: The Century Co., 1932), 113, 114, and 121.

214.   Frederick Charles Dietz, *English Public Finance 1558-1641* (London: The Century Co., 1932), 118.

1643, An Ordinance for the speedy Rising and Leavy-
ing of Moneys, set by way of Charge or new Impost, on
the severall Commodities mentioned in the Schedule
hereunto annexed was intended to be a temporary
measure: an excise tax—a duty on manufactured
goods imposed at the point of manufacture rather
than from the point of sale. It was supposed to be
renewable on a month-to-month basis.[215] Distilled spirits were not included in the first excise
schedule. But a few months later, on 8 September
1643, the scheme was amended in *An Ordinance*
for the speedy Raising and Leavying of Moneys by
way of Charge and New-Impost, upon the severall
Commodities, in a Schedule hereunto annexed con-
tained, as well for the better securing of Trade, as for
the maintenance of the Forces raised for the defence of
the King, Parliament, and Kingdom, both by Sea and
Land, as for and towards the payment of the Debts of
the Commonwealth, for which the Publike Faith is, or
shall be ingaged, adding a 2s 4d (about £14 today)

---

215.   Great Britain, *An Ordinance for the speedy Rising and Leavy-*
ing of Moneys, set by way of Charge or new Impost, on the severall Com-
modities mentioned in the Schedule hereunto annexed, 22 July 1643
(London: HMSO).

per 36-gallon barrel excise on 'strong water and *aqua vitæ* made or distilled within the realm' which the Company dutifully collected from its member-distillers.[216]

By then, spirits were a valuable commodity on par with beer and ale. Yet the burden of payment for the spirits excise rested on distillers' shoulders until 17 March 1654, when *An Ordinance for Continuing the Excise* was passed and saddled sellers with this financial obligation.[217] Historian John Chartres determined from the Treasury's excise reports for that year, 80,000 gallons of taxable spirits were produced and consumed, while the same reports showed that roughly 41,000,000 gallons of excised beer were produced and con-

---

216.   Great Britain, *An Ordinance for the speedy Raising and Leavy-ing of Moneys by way of Charge and New-Impost, upon the severall Commodities, in a Schedule hereunto annexed contained, as well for the better securing of Trade, as for the maintenance of the Forces raised for the defence of the King, Parliament, and Kingdom, both by Sea and Land, as for and towards the payment of the Debts of the Common-wealth, for which the Publike Faith is, or shall be ingaged*, 8 September 1643 (London: HMSO).

217.   Great Britain, *An Ordinance for Continuing the Excise*, 17 March 1654 (London: HMSO).

sumed.[218] Responsibility for payment of the spirits excise reverted to the distillers on 25 December 1660 when *A Grant of certain Impositions upon Beer, Ale, and other Liquors, for the Increase of his Majesty's Revenue during his Life* raised the rate to 5s 8d (about £30 today) per 36-gallon barrel on spirits 'distilled within the realm from foreign or domestic materials'.[219] Be warned: The production figures used here do not reflect the quantities of unexcised beer and spirits produced during this period by rogue distillers and brewers. Since there are no accurate accountings for this unregulated production and consumption, these statistics only present a very limited portrait of what was actually manufactured during the period. We could drag you through the fiscal roller-coaster that English brewers and distillers rode between the 1640s

---

218.   John Chartres, 'No English Calvados? English distillers and the cider industry in the seventeenth and eighteenth centuries?', *English rural society 1500-1800: Essays in honour of Joan Thirsk*, ed. by John Chartres and David Hey (Cambridge: Cambridge University Press, 1990), 316; British Library, Lansdowne MS 1215, fol. 7. The beer figure is based on the £113,842 15s 3d in excise that was collected by excise men at 2s per 36-gallon barrel.

219.   Great Britain, *A Grant of certain Impositions upon Beer, Ale, and other Liquors, for the Increase of his Majesty's Revenue during his Life*, 1660 (12 Charles II, c.23) (London: HMSO).

and 1680s. But we won't. Historians John Chartres and William Ashworth did a great job of unpacking that nightmare of numbers. You can read their accounts on your own time, if you're curious.

So, let's jump ahead to when William of Orange and Queen Mary ascended the English throne in 1688. Three major changes shifted consumer preference from beer to spirits predicated on affordability which was only one piece to this puzzle. The first transition transpired with the passage of an amended statute titled *An act for an additional duty of excise upon beer, ale, and other liquors* which not only raised the spirits excise to 7s 8d (about £44 today) per 36-gallon barrel, it shifted the burden of payment once again from distillers to spirits sellers.[220] According to the excise returns for 1684 through 1688 from England and Wales, the average quantity of spirits excised was over 533,000 gallons—a roughly 660 per cent leap in output when compared to thirty

---

220. 1 William & Mary, c.24.

years earlier in the 1654 returns.[221] (During the same period, an average of 27,900,000 gallons of beer was excised, representing about a 30 per cent decline when compared to the 1654 returns.[222]) Although taxation cost spirits sellers as well as beer retailers—and consequently their customers—more than a few major price hikes, England's social drinking culture embraced spirits drinking so much that only beer appeared on the surface to suffer from rising taxation. This, of course, does not consider the quantities of unexcised beer that were also consumed.

Since the excise scheme's inception, in 1643, beer was more significantly slapped in its financial face than spirits when the tax was amortised across the number of servings per 36-gallon barrel. For example, with the new tax increase imposed on 20 March 1690, charged brewers 7s

---

221.   John Chartres, 'No English Calvados? English distillers and the cider industry in the seventeenth and eighteenth centuries?', *English rural society 1500-1800: Essays in honour of Joan Thirsk*, ed. by John Chartres and David Hey (Cambridge: Cambridge University Press, 1990), 316; Custom House MS, 'Excise Revenue Accounts, 1662-1827', 255-256.

222.   TNA: T64/172, 22.

18d (about £51 today) per 288 pints of strong beer or 0.35d (about 0.18p today) per pint. [223] Distillers, on the other hand, were charged 15s 4d (about £92 today) per 36,864 drams (the measure at which spirits were sold, especially in dram shops and hot water houses) or 0.0049d (about 0.003p today) per dram. However, this economic advantage did not stop distillers from registering their complaints over the tax increase.

As we mentioned earlier, *The Distiller of London* expressly prohibited the distilling of 'unwholesome Sugarwaters' by its member-distillers even though they sweentened their rectification with sugar. This posed a problem for the planters in the British Caribbean colonies, especially those in Barbados. The concern wasn't the sugar refinement business that developed, it was the importation and selling of molasses to English distillers for mixing with grain spirits to bulk out quantities and reduce the cost of goods sold. The Company expressed its displeasure with the introduction of a bill to the House of Commons

223.   2 William & Mary, c.9 (19).

that would inadvertently encourage the adultera-
tion of grain spirits, which was against one of the
Company's primary tenets. The petition, dated 30
December 1690, stated that:

> But if the said Bill does pass into an
> Act It is impossible to effect the said
> design of the consumption of Corne
> it not being possible to drawe a
> spirit from Corne without a Mixture
> of some other material and besides
> it will considerably lessen their Maj-
> esties Revenue and also utterly ruin
> and impoverish several thousands of
> their Majesties subjects and the Art
> and trade of Distilling in England to
> the Inriching for a time such par-
> ticular persons as have ...quantity
> of French Brandy in their hands as
> your Petitioners are ready to make
> appeare to your Lordshipps if you
> will vouchsafe to permit them to be
> heard thereto.[224]

---

224.   Parliamentary Archives: HL/PO/JO/10/1/431/375.

The British Caribbean colonies' sugar planters likewise petitioned the House of Commons, refuting that:

> The said Sugar Plantations, which are already loaded with great Duties, and by the present Warn are brought to very great distress, will be so much discouraged, that other Nations, who are rivals with us in that Trade, and use all meanes to make it easier to their Subjects, will have the advantage of us, and in time beat us out of it.
>
> The West India Navigation which breeds up to many Seamen, and employs so great a number of Ships, will be much abated.
>
> Many Thousands whose employment depends upon refining Sugars in England will be ruined, as also many in the said Sugar Plantations.
>
> This said act will not answer the Ends proposed thereby to encrease the expense of Corn, but will encourage the clandestine importation of Foreign Brandy.[225]

---

225.   Parliamentary Archives: HL/PO/JO/10/1/431/375(a).

Funny thing is: In *An Act for the Encourage-*
ing the Distilling of Brandy and Spirits from Come and
for laying severall Dutyes on Low Wines or Spirits of
the first Extraction, Parliament specifically banned
adding molasses wash to grain spirits which was
in effect from 24 December 1690 to 25 December 1695.[226] However, it was not easily enforced.
So, the sugar planters and distillers who were not
Company members inadvertently had their way.
The following year, in 1691, Treasury reports show
that 144,135 gallons of low wines from molasses
were distilled for further recitification. By 1699,
that quantity increased to 939,083 gallons while
the production of low wines from malted grain
stood at 1,620,496 gallons.[227]

Although it was geared to favour spirits
over beer, the intentional change in the excise
rates was coupled with the passage on 25 December 1695 of a statute titled *An Act for the Encourag-*
ing the Distilling of Brandy and Spirits from Corne
and for laying several Dutyes on Low Wines of Spir-

---

226.   1 William & Mary, c.34

227.   The National Archives (hereinafter TNA): T64/172, 26.

its of the First Extraction that triggered two meaningful changes.[228] First, all charters and letters patent granted for the distillation of spirits were declared null and void. This meant the Worshipful Company of Distillers no longer managed the city's legitimate distilling trade and all monopolies and patents including those owned by de Mayerne, Cademan, and Brouncker were invalidated. (Although, historian Peter Clark believed the Company lost its control on the trade after 1689.[229]) It also meant that the ban on street selling and the retailing of spirits to inns, hostels, taverns, alehouses, victualling houses and other places in which social drinking was lifted after the Company had controlled these sorts of sales for 56 years in its 1639 ordinances (see page 156). Bottom line: Anyone could make and sell spirits to anyone without any ties to a Company-sanctioned distillery. Second, the statute discouraged the importation of French wheat and wine while

---

228.   1 William & Mary, c.34.

229.   Peter Clark, 'The "Mother Gin" Controversy in the Early Eighteenth Century', *Transactions of the Royal Historical Society*, 38 (1988), 64.

it encouraged distillers and brewers to exploit the surplus grain yield that resulted from a series of abundant harvests during the 1690s. But with the excise's heavy hit on pricing, distillers gained the economic upper hand.

A Treasury excise report titled 'The Number of Common Brewers & Victuallers in the whole Kingdom with the Amount in Barrels of strong and small charg'd in the several years below', showed that from a total of 181,595,196 gallons of excisable beer produced in 1687, the total dropped to 119,861,928 gallons by 1693 and dropped again to 107,044,668 gallons in 1699, representing a 60 per cent decline over the course of thirteen years.[230] But from a total of 516,402 gallons of spirits in 1687, the quantity almost doubled to 948,376 gallons in 1693. But then, it decreased to 877,085 gallons by 1699, representing an over 60 per cent increase during the same thirteen-year period.[231] But what really precipitated this change

---

230.   TNA: T64/172, 22.

231.   TNA: T64/172, 25.

in consumer habits that consequently impeded production?

As historian Roy Porter pointed out, 'for a while at least—the early Georgian "pudding time"—saw agricultural improvements make produce abundant and gin dead cheap.'[232] This is the moment that Tlusty noted in which historians 'of both Germany and England have described a process...in which gin began as the drink of choice for the upper circles of society, then declined in status over time, until both the drinkers and distributors belonged to the lowest socioeconomic levels.'[233] Porter further agreed with historian Hans Mendick, who argued that with the continued rise of conspicuous consumption in eighteenth-century London, gin drinking 'functioned as a vehicle of plebeian self-consciousness' which he believed should be interpreted as 'a claim on the part of ple-

---

232.   Roy Porter, 'Consumption: disease of the consumer society', *Consumption and the World of Goods*, ed. by John Brewer and Roy Porter (London: Routledge, 1993), 59.

233.   B. Ann Tlusty, 'Water of Life, Water of Death: The Controversy over Brandy and Gin in Early Modern Augsburg,' *Central European History*, 31/1 (1998), 5.

beians to be as good as their so-called betters.'[234]

(Ah, keeping up with Joneses at its finest level.) Historian John Styles corroborated with these conclusions, adding that with increased wages, the labouring poor's capacity to respond to 'accessible innovations' also grew commensurately as 'the penetration of this market by gin...demonstrated the willingness of poor consumers to substitute new commodities for old'—such as gin for beer.[235] But as one observer in 1737 noted 'dram-drinking has been a practise among the poor sort because they could be made merry with distilled spirits cheaper than they could with any other liquor.'[236] (Bottom line: The poor drank spirits regardless of fad or fashion. It was a dirt cheap buzz.) While progressions and regressions in the development of early modern English distilla-

---

234.   Peter Burke, '*Res et verba*: conspicuous consumption in the early modern world,', , *Consumption and the World of Goods*, ed. by John Brewer and Roy Porter (London: Routledge, 1993), 150.

235.   John Styles, 'Manufacturing, consumption and design in eighteenth-century England', *Consumption and the World of Goods*, ed. by John Brewer and Roy Porter (London: Routledge, 1993), 538.

236.   Peter Clark, 'The "Mother Gin" Controversy in the Early Eighteenth Century', *Transactions of the Royal Historical Society*, 38 (1988), 65.

tion seemingly hit a rising trajectory based on the 'fear of missing out' (FOMO) aspirations of the middling sorts and labouring poor, there were other factors that influenced the English palate. The change—for better or for worse—fell in step with the technological and scientific advancement that highlighted England's Age of Enlightenment (1685-1815). What resulted from this lowering of standards and the rise of modern production methods is the subject of our next chapter.

CHAPTER SIX

'...SUCH MIXT AND CONFUS'D TRASH...'

There were no eight 'gin acts' in the 1700s. And the Gin Craze? That was tabloid puffery, written to sell more newspapers and keep the temperance folks happy.

AMID THE POLITICAL and economic chaos generated by the seventeenth-century inception of the excise scheme, the cancellation of monopolies such as the Worshipful Company of Distillers in 1695, and the Crown's campaign to push for distillation from grain, distillers proposed expansions of their manufacturing processes, freeing them from the Company's restrictions. For example, Isaac Crabbe, Abraham (John) Bayly, Isaac Bennett, and Arthur Evans filed Patent #362 on 10 April 1699 for:

> ...a way never practiced or used by
> any of drawing low wines and spirits
> from turnepps, carrotts, parsnepps
> sufficient in quantitity and quality
> both for the consumption within,
> and trade of this our Kingdome,
> which are much cheaper and better
> than any distilled from corne.[237]

This patent suggested doing precisely what the Company hoped to prevent: the distillation of English spirits from anything other than English grain. Similarly, William Stammers filed Patent #504 on 4 November 1728 for his invention of:

> ...a new ingredient by which he
> can ameliorate or rectify spirits
> drawn from malt, molasses, and
> other liquors in such a manner as
> will render them safe and pleasant,

237.   Frederic Arthur Filby, *A History of Food Adulteration and Analysis* (London: G. Allen & Unwin Limited, 1934), 158; Great Britain, *Titles of Patents of Invention Chronologically arranged From March 2, 1617 (14 James I.) to October 1, 1852 (16 Victoriæ): Part I, Nos. 1 to 4,800, pages 1 to 784*, ed. by Bennett Woodcroft (London: HMSO, 1854), 67.

William Hogarth's 1751 engraving titled 'Beer Street and Gin Lane' is only one example of the anti-gin propaganda issued during the so-called Gin Craze (Source: private collection).

and equally wholesome with French brandy...[238]

His intent was to improve on 'common methods now in use for rectifying spirits, i.e. *aqua fortis*, spirit of vitriol, and unwholesome ingredients are extremely pernicious to the subject.' However, this distilling of English spirits from molasses or sugar was another activity banned by the Company who had spent the greater part of 1695 locking horns with British Caribbean sugar planters in petitions to Parliament. Without their intervention, new ideas such as these arose without standardised restrictions.

By now you are asking yourself, where's the gin? Until the eighteenth century, 'gin' was not the commonplace term for juniper-berry forward spirits. So, who coined the word 'gin'? Satirist, physician, and political economist Bernard de Mandeville, in 1714, first used the term in a pub-

---

238.   Frederic Arthur Filby, *A History of Food Adulteration and Analysis* (London: G. Allen & Unwin Limited, 1934), 158; Great Britain, *Titles of Patents of Invention Chronologically arranged From March 2, 1617 (14 James I.) to October 1, 1852 (16 Victoriæ): Part I, Nos. 1 to 4,800, pages 1 to 784*, ed. by Bennett Woodcroft (London: HMSO, 1854), 92.

lished work titled *The Fable of the Bees: Or, Private Vices, Publick Benefits*, in which he lamented that:

> …the infamous liquor, the name
> of which, derived from Juniper in
> Dutch, is now, by frequent use, and
> the laconic spirit of the nation, from
> a word of middling-length, shrunk
> into a monosyllable, intoxicating
> gin, that charms the unactive, the
> desperate and crazy of either sex,
> and makes the starving sot behold
> his rags and nakedness with stu-
> pid indolence, or banter both in
> senseless laughter, and more insipid
> jests![239]

Consisting of a poem previously pub-lished in 1705 under the title *The Grumbling Hive, or Knaves Turn'd Honest*; an essay on 'An Enquiry into the Origin of Moral Virtue'; and a commen-tary called 'Remarks', de Mandeville's remarks suggested the term 'gin' was only attributed to the wholly unregulated English spirit that was

---

239.   Bernard de Mandeville, *The Fable of Bees: Or, Private Vices, Publick Benefits* (London: J. Roberts, 1714), 46.

produced by distillers who had not and were not managed by the Worshipful Company of Distillers.

But it was journalist and pamphleteer Daniel Defoe who, on behalf of the Worshipful Company of Distillers, identified in a pamphlet printed in 1725 that the cheap gin producer was:

> a sort of petty distiller who made up those compound waters from such mixt and confus'd Trash, as they could get to work from... The spirits they drew were foul and gross; but they mixed them up with such additions as they could get, to make them palatable.[240]

Defoe concluded this assault by adding that rogue distillers 'had found out a way to hit the palate of the poor by their new-fashioned compound water called Geneva.'[241] Thus, while the

---

240. Daniel Defoe, *A Brief Case of the Distillers, and of the Distilling Trade in England, shewing how far it is the interest of England to encourage the said trade, as it is so considerable an advantage to the landed interest, to the trade and navigation, to the publick revenue, and to the employment of the poor. Humbly recommended to the Lords and Commons of Great Britain, in the present Parliament assembled.* (London: Thomas Warner, 1725), 18-19.

241. Daniel Defoe, *The Novels and Miscellaneous Works of Daniel De Foe* (London: D.A. Tallboys, 1840), 220.

aristocracy and middling sorts enjoyed the rectified offerings of the Company's distillers, a proliferation of dram shops and 'hot water houses'
offered the labouring poor and the unemployed
poor cheaper, compounded alternatives that were
produced by unregulated rogue distillers.[242] What
were the compound waters that Defoe mentioned?
And what was eighteenth-century geneva when
compared with its seventeenth-century predeces-
sors? First of all, by this time, the terms geneva
and gin were loosely interchangeable in the same
fashion that the words beer and ale were bantered about in early modern English writings. In
truth, both brews were produced in hopped and
unhopped versions. During the fifteenth through
eighteenth centuries there were unhopped beers
and hopped ales produced despite earlier historians incorrectly affirming fifteenth-century
physician Andrew Boorde's proclamation that 'Ale
is made of malte and water' and 'Bere is made of

242.   Peter Clark, 'The "Mother Gin" Controversy in the Early
Eighteenth Century, *Transactions of the Royal Historical Society*, 28
(1988), 65.

malte, hoppes, and water.'[243] By similar thinking, the same can be said for the eighteenth-century usage of the terms geneva and gin.

The 1752 volume of *Medical Essays and Observations* noted that, in 1735:

> the Gin commonly sold in **London**, is made by distilling 30 Gallons of Water, 10 Gallons of Lamp-spirits [meaning either methanol or ethanol], and a Quart of Oil of Turpentine.[244]

This so-called gin was compounded rather than rectified, combining 'lamp-spirit' (the stuff used in alcohol lamps) that was possibly distilled from molasses or fermented fruit flavoured with essential oils or infused with dried botanicals without the benefit of redistillation. Author of a publican and spirits retailer guide that was pub-

---

243.   Andrew Boorde, *The Fryst Boke of the Introduction of Knowledge Made by Andrew Boorde of Physyche Doctor*, ed. by F.J. Furnivall (London: N. Trübner & Com 1870), 256.

244.   A Society in Edinburgh, 'LXXVIII. An Account of the most remarkable Improvement and Discoveries in Physick made or proposed since the Beginning of the Year 1735', *Medical Essays and Observations*, Vol. V (Edinburgh: Hamilton, Balfour, and Neill, 1752), 426.

lished in six editions between 1797 and 1800, Patrick Boyle also contributed a compounded method for making twenty gallons of gin plus a recipe for making gin bitters.[245] His compounded gin recipe contained several ingredients that are now considered to be poisonous, reading that:

FOR TWENTY GALLONS OF GIN

Sixteen gallons of spirits one to five under proof. Take one penny weight and three quarters of the oil of vitriol, one penny weight and a half of the oil of almonds, two penny weights of the oil of juniper berries, mixed with lump sugar and spirits of wine as before: add to it one pint of lime water, use the whole. After you dissolved five pounds of lump sugar in two gallons and a half of water, that has boiled as before directed, fine it down with the proportioned quantity of allum and salt of tartar.

It is noticed, that a handful of borage

---

245.   Patrick Boyle, *The publican and spirit dealers' Daily Companion.* Sixth edition (London: Patrick Boyle, 1800), 26-27.

> will give, if steeped in the gin, when
> first prepared a fine flavor.
>
> To make lime water, you take six
> pounds of unslacked [sic] lime, put
> it into a pail; take about one pint of
> water, which will dissolve the lime.
> When it is dissolved, add one gallon
> of water to it, and stir up the lime,
> when it is cold and well settled, it is
> then fit for use. [246]

The unslaked lime used to make the lime water for this recipe is also known as calcium oxide, burnt lime, or quicklime—a highly caustic substance which is produced by calcinating or burning limestone in kilns. When mixed with water its caustic properties are reduced. Limewater is more familiarly used today in the preparation of maize or masa harina, using a process called nixtamalization which makes the niacin (vitamin B-3) in the grain nutritionally accessible. At this point, what Boyle termed as being a gin had more in common with Water of Juniper (see page

---

246.   Patrick Boyle, *The publican and spirit dealers' Daily Companion*. Sixth edition (London: Patrick Boyle, 1800), 26-27.

133) than with modern-day gin. But in the same book, Boyle applied the term 'gin' to a recipe for a digestive bitters, which he called Fine Gin Bitters.

The first patent medicine to be produced in England, apothecary Richard Stoughton was granted Patent #390, on 3 April 1712, to produce a 'restorative cordial' that went by the various names of Stoughton's Elixir Magnum Stomachicum, The Great Cordial Elixir, and The Stomatick Tincture or Bitter Drops.[247] This new digestive aid was an overwhelming success in England and in the British North American colonies, until the 1776 American Revolutionary War unleashed an embargo on British imports and the rise of American copycat products to meet colonial demand. By that time, producers could find Stoughton's recipe in books like the 1808 *Pharmacopoeia* of the Massachusetts Medical Society.[248] The popularity attributed to

247. Great Britain, *Titles of Patents of Invention Chronologically arranged From March 2, 1617 (14 James I.) to October 1, 1852 (16 Victoriæ): Part I, Nos. 1 to 4,800, pages 1 to 784*, ed. by Bennett Woodcroft (London: HMSO, 1854), 71.

248. George B. Griffenhagen and James Harvey, 'Old English Patent Medicines in America', *Contributions from the Museum of History and Techonology*, Paper 10 (1959), 67.

digestive bitters extended from the apothecary to the public house, especially when married with a familiar spirit category such as gin as seen in Boyle's recipe for fine gin bitters:

TO MAKE FINE GIN BITTERS

Steep for ten days, in thirteen gallons of fine spirits, one to five under proof, half an ounce of coriander seeds, half an ounce of almond cake, two ounces of virgin snake root: then after the above is steeped and taken out, take and pound it in a mortar, adding to it a quarter of an ounce of oil of orange, a quarter of an ounce of the oil of carraway, a quarter of an ounce of oil of wormwood, with a small quantity of spirits, until it becomes an oil; put to the above three gallons of spirits, with thirteen quarts of water that has boiled, and it will produce fourteen gallons and two quarts, superior in quality to any generally sold.[249]

---

249. Patrick Boyle, *The publican and spirit dealers' Daily Companion*. Sixth edition (London: Patrick Boyle, 1800), 27.

There were purists who continued to follow the old ways, making Juniper Water and calling it that. It was produced without any embellishments—aside from sugar. For example, distiller George Smith in the 1738 edition of his book *A Compleat Body of Distilling, Explaining the Mysteries of that Science* gave a simple formula, which he described as being 'more in esteem (as has been observ'd in the former part of this work) especially amongst the populace, than all the whole tribe of distill'd waters put together.'[250] The recipe called to:

> Take best Juniper berries twelve ounces, proof spirits three gallons, Water q.s. Distill and dulcify with Sugar one pound, for sale or use.[251]

Similarly, Juniper Water as a medicinal preparation continued to appear in popular publications such as William Allen's 1753 edition of *The*

---

250.   George Smith, *A Compleat Body of Distilling, Explaining the Mysteries of that Science in a most easy and familiar Manner* (London: Henry Lintot, 1738), 138.

251.   George Smith, *A Compleat Body of Distilling, Explaining the Mysteries of that Science in a most easy and familiar Manner* (London: Henry Lintot, 1738), 138.

New Dispensatory, which included a formula that he recommended not only as a carminative to relieve flatulence, but as an after-dinner cordial.[252] This formula instructed to:

> Take of
> Juniper berries, one pound;
> Sweet fennel seeds,
> Caraway seeds, each an ounce and
> a half;
> Proof spirit, one gallon;
> Water as much as sufficient to pre-
> vent burning.
> Distill off one gallon.[253]

Gin, geneva, Juniper Water, *aqua fructum*—whatever name distillers, retailers, and writers threw around—these juniper-forward spirits were linked in the history books with the chaotic drinking culture known as the Gin Craze (1720-1751) without making any distinction about their contents or their drinking audience. The events surrounding the Gin Craze have been muddled,

---

252.   William Lewis, *The New Dispensatory* (London: J. Nourse, 1753), 381.

253.   William Lewis, *The New Dispensatory* (London: J. Nourse, 1753), 381.

mashed, and mangled by historians Jessica Warner, John Chartres, and Constance Anne Wilson, amongst others. For example, Warner postulated that this Gin Craze consumption frenzy was not affected by the economic shifts that impacted all social groups—particularly the lower middling sorts and the poor—noting that the 'calamitous drop in real wages that occurred in the second half of the [eighteenth] century had no more effect on consumption than did the gains that occurred in the first half…'[254] She further added that the 'gin craze followed the trajectory of other and more recent drug epidemics: that is, it lasted for the span of one generation.'[255] In other words, she felt the Gin Craze was just a trend that came and went out of fashion.

John Chartres suggested that politics, more than economics, played a role in the Gin Craze's inception, noting that 'there is even evidence to suggest that in the absence of war and protec-

---

254. Jessica Warner, *Craze: Gin and Debauchery in an Age of Reason* (London: Profile Book, 2004), 208.

255. Jessica Warner, *Craze: Gin and Debauchery in an Age of Reason* (London: Profile Book, 2004), 208.

tion, there may have been no "age of gin".'[256] He supported his conclusion by noting that despite 'continuing low prices for grain, at least compared with those of the 1720s, the years 1731-3 saw a great resurgence of brandy imports' after the 1729 Treaty of Seville and the 1731 Treaty of Vienna.[257] Thus, when British spirits production declined in the early 1750s, 'the share of brandy in the home market again increased, as did the absolute level of imports'.[258] Therefore, in Chartres' opinion, the Gin Craze was instigated by tensions and hostilities coming from all corners. But considering England's involvement in foreign wars throughout the eighteenth century, it does not explain how the

---

256. John Chartres, 'No English Calvados? English distillers and the cider industry in the seventeenth and eighteenth centuries?', *English rural society 1500-1800: Essays in honour of Joan Thirsk*, ed. by John Chartres and David Hey (Cambridge: Cambridge University Press, 1990), 325.

257. John Chartres, 'No English Calvados? English distillers and the cider industry in the seventeenth and eighteenth centuries?', *English rural society 1500-1800: Essays in honour of Joan Thirsk*, ed. by John Chartres and David Hey (Cambridge: Cambridge University Press, 1990), 325.

258. John Chartres, 'No English Calvados? English distillers and the cider industry in the seventeenth and eighteenth centuries?', *English rural society 1500-1800: Essays in honour of Joan Thirsk*, ed. by John Chartres and David Hey (Cambridge: Cambridge University Press, 1990), 325.

'age of gin' ended amid the continued political and economic turmoil.

Wilson concluded that because 'distilling was forbidden totally during certain periods in the 1750s, due to bad harvests and the need to convert grain into foodstuffs' the distilling trade was interrupted, thus ending the Gin Craze.[259] Wilson's deduction is debatable, which we detail later in this chapter. Did the Gin Craze really have a significant impact on beer consumption? That's hard to confirm because by 1700, Peter Clark told us that 'spirits were drunk with or after beer (as a chaser) or mixed with wine and spices to make punch'.[260] Punch was a term that was bantered around not only in the eighteenth century, but well into the nineteenth century, when more fruity tickled the palate, such as the recipe served in London's Garrick Club:

---

259.   Constance Anne Wilson, *Water of Life: A History of Wine-Distilling and Spirits 500 BC to AD 2000* (Totnes, Devon: Prospect Books, 2006), 226.

260.   Peter Clark, *The English Alehouse: A Social History 1200-1830* (Burnt Mill: Longman Group, 1983) 213.

GARRICK CLUB GIN PUNCH
Pour a half pint of gin on the outer peel of a lemon, then a little lemon juice, a glass of maraschino, about a pint and a quarter of water, and two bottles of iced soda-water. [261]

Alehouses throughout the kingdom served whatever the customer wanted. And if that call included ale, beer, brandy, cider, punch, and spirits, so be it. So the big question is: What really precipitated the Gin Craze's alleged decline?

Let's revisit the eight alleged 'gin acts' passed by Parliament that some historians use as the pattern for explaining the ramp-up to the end of the Gin Craze. Did the impact—or lack thereof—of these acts really contribute to changing eighteenth-century English spirits drinking? Or was something else responsible for curbing or simply changing the consumption of inebriants in England? First, we must let you know that these statutes were not specifically directed to manage gin or geneva production and sales. They were

---

261. Anonymous, 'Christmas Miscellany', *The Era Sunday*, 30 December 1838, 164.

aimed at controlling the overall category of 'British spirits', combining English and Irish spirits in legal terms, thus allowing Parliament to introduce a tax, in 1661, on whiskey production. (Next, the Malt Tax, passed in 1725, married Scottish whisky production to the rest of the 'British spirits' umbrella.)

When the first 'gin act'—*An Act for laying Duty upon Compound Water or Spirits; and for licensing the Retailers thereof*—was passed on 25 December 1729, the statute raised the excise on spirits to £9 (about £516 today) per 36-gallon barrel and ordered retailers to pay an annual licence of £20 (about £2,355 today).[262] However, pay attention to the fact that this law targeted the compounders of spirits, not the rectifiers. The compounders merely blended essential oils into spirit or infused botanicals into spirit. They did not rectify spirits. The Treasury's excise reports show that about 4,708,774 gallons of excised spirits were produced that year plus 126,233,028 gallons of beer.[263] A

---

262.   2 George II, c. 17.

263.   TNA: T64/172, 22.

retailer had to take out an annual licence for £20 (about £2,355 today). However, only a few hundred people did.[264]

When the second 'gin act' —*An Act for repealing an Act for laying a Duty on Compound Water or Spirits, and for licensing the Retailers thereof; and for determining certain Duties on French Brandy, and for granting other Duties in Lieu; and for enforcing the laws for preventing the Running of Brandies*— was passed on 24 June 1733, it repealed the excise charges from the first 'gin act' passed in 1729, and it encouraged the exportation of 'spirits drawn from British Corn, without Mixture of other Materials' as a means of reducing local consumption.[265] Parliament reckoned that if the English spirits left English shores for other places like the British North American colonies, English drinkers would have less spirits to drink at home. Plus, the Treasury could still collect excise on the spirits that the distillers produced. The Treasury's excise reports

---

264.   Peter Clark, 'The "Mother Gin" Controversy in the Early Eighteenth Century', *Transactions of the Royal Historical Society*, 38 (1988), 66.

265.   6 George II, c. 17.

showed that spirits sales rose only marginally to 4,821,434 gallons while beer production increased to 138,687,516 gallons.[266] But historian Peter Clark noted that this repeal 'encouraged a major revival of home production and consumption.'[267] (Get out the old still, honey. We're makin' our own—again!)

Next, the third 'gin act'—*An Act for Laying a Duty upon the Retailers of Spirituous Liquors; and for licensing the Retailers thereof*—passed on 5 May 1736 mandated that retailers and distillers who sold directly to consumers had to acquire an annual licence of £50 (about £5,890 today) to sell 'any Quantity less than a gallon'.[268] This hefty fee burdened the sellers instead of the producers. That didn't stop spirits manufacture, which shot up to 6,116,314 gallons that year, while beer declined slightly to 134,020,960 gallons.[269] That seemingly did not hinder the 7,044 spirits retailers of

---

266.   TNA: T64/172, 22 and 25.

267.   Peter Clark, 'The "Mother Gin" Controversy in the Early Eighteenth Century', *Transactions of the Royal Historical Society,* 38 (1988), 67.

268.   9 George II, c. 23.

269.   TNA: T62/172, 22 and 25.

William Hogarth's depiction of a hanging at London's Tyburn Tree with a female street seller dispensing gin (upper right) while another hawker offers gingerbread (lower right) which was commonly served with gin, circa 1747 (Source: private collection).

which only 3,835 sold gin and brandy alone—the remainder were already licenced separately as victuallers.[270]

The next year, the fourth 'gin act'—*An Act for repealing the present Duty on Sweets, and for granting a less Duty thereupon and for explaining and enforcing*

---

270.   Peter Clark, 'The "Mother Gin" Controversy in the Early Eighteenth Century', *Transactions of the Royal Historical Society*, 38 (1988), 68.

the Execution of an Act passed in the Ninth Year of his present Majesty's Reign intituled, An Act for laying a Duty upon the Retailers of Spirituous Liquors, and for licensing the Retailers thereof; and for appropriating the Supplies granted in this Session of Parliament; and for making forth Duplicates of Exchequer Bills, Lottery Tickets and Orders, lost, burnt or otherwise destroyed (aka: the Sweets Act)—passed on 21 June 1737 which we had mentioned earlier, repealed the 36s (about £212 today) per 36-gallon barrel excise charge on the dulcified liquors produced by Company member-distillers and imposed a new charge of 12s (about £70 today) per barrel—or 4d (about £2 today) per gallon—on 'sweets'—a 66 per cent discount from the previous rate.[271] However, there are no Treasury excise reports that document the quantities of 'sweets' produced in England during this period as opposed to other spirits. The statute additionally authorised regional excise commissioners to reward informers who reported the activities of unlicenced street sellers who were mostly poor women, immigrants,

---

271.   10 George II, c. 17.

and the destitute who sold their wares from barrows, stalls, and small boats.[272] This action led to informers being attacked on London streets by mobs who disagreed with the law, as noted in the preamble of the next statute.[273]

Gin was not always sold alone. There are some visual clues to the popularity of this pairing. The first comes from William Hogarth, the satirist and artist who campaigned against the consumption of gin in his 1751 *Gin Lane* engraving. One of Hogarth's other impactful presentations titled *Industry and Idleness*, consisted of 12 engravings that related a story about the rewards of diligence and hard labour as well as the disastrous end that could befall a youth who was lazy. The eleventh plate depicts the idle apprentice at his execution on the Tyburn Tree, situated near in what is now known as Marble Arch (see page 205). Look to the right of the image. There is a baker wearing

---

272. Peter Clark, 'The "Mother Gin" Controversy in the Early Eighteenth Century', *Transactions of the Royal Historical Society,* 38 (1988), 69.

273. Peter Clark, 'The "Mother Gin" Controversy in the Early Eighteenth Century', *Transactions of the Royal Historical Society,* 38 (1988), 81.

an apron and selling round balls of gingerbread. Behind him there is a cart from which a woman is selling drams of gin. The pairing caused concern amongst the better sorts because it was associated with the poor and social disorder.

Hangings were not the only social gathering in which gin and gingerbread appeared according to an item in the 10 June 1788 *Kentish Gazette*. In London's Hyde Park, 'Kate the retailer of gin and gingerbread' sold her wares as she strolled passed chimney sweeps, dukes, and even the Duchess of Gordon, this pairing offered a poor young maid a less nefarious way to make her way in the metropolis. At the the executions of 'Maw the Soldier' and 'Morat the Black' at the Shepherd's Bush hanging tree in West London according to a notice in the *Derby Mercury* newspaper from 10 March 1736:

> There were several Gallons of Gin sold on that Road all Sunday, notionally by Running Distillers with Bottles, but almost every 100 yards was a Stall with Gingerbread and Gin.

A similar note appeared in *The Scots* magazine in the 1 February 1744 edition that these items were also sold along the roadside:

> ...the poorest retailer, even those who sell gin and ginger-bread in baskets upon the highway, will always find money or credit for two gallons, which amounts to but three shillings...

The refreshment was also a common treat at London's Frost Fairs which took place from 1650 through 1814. The brutal winters brought on by the Little Ice Age inspired Londoners to gather on the River Thames when it froze over to enjoy entertainments, shopping, and the warmth of gin and gingerbread. Neighbouring booths were advertised on a map titled 'Mrs Mary Malkinton' that was 'printed on the ice' on 2 January 1715. The Gingerbread Stall was situated at location 'K' in the legend and the Geneva Booth was only separated from its usual companion by a stall that sold roasted mutton shoulder.

But what sort of gingerbread recipe was this? Was it one that is familiar to our modern-day palate which used a number of ingredients that were unaffordable to poor bakers let alone to poor consumers. A recipe found in Gervase Markham's *Country Contentment or The English Hus-wife*:

TO MAKE COURSE GINGER BREAD

To make course Ginger bread, take a quart of honie and set it on the coales and refine it: then take a penny worth of ginger, as much pepper, as much Licoras; and a quarter of a pound of Aniseedes, and a penny worth of Saunders: All of these must be beaten and searsed, and so put into the hony: then put in a quarter of a pint of Claret wine or old ale: then take three penny Manchets finely grated and strow it amongst the rest, and stirre it till it

come to a stiff Past, and then make
it into Cakes and drie them gently.[274]

A more plausible recipe style for a poor
man's gingerbread was discovered by the National
Trust. Even though it is attributed to the Victorian
era, the ingredients and method are much more
to the fashion of a treat that baker could whip up
overnight and hawk at a hanging the next day:

POOR MAN'S GINGERBREAD

225 gr plain flour
225 gr butter (or other fat), soft-
ened
15-30 grams ground ginger, depend-
ing on your taste preference
170 gr dark treacle
a splash of milk

Place the butter and flour into a
bowl.

Heat the treacle and milk in a
small saucepan until it is very hot.

Pour into the flour mixture and

---

274.   Gervase Markham, *Countrey contentments, in two bookes: the
first, containing the whole art of riding great horses ... with the breeding, breaking, dyeting and ordring of them ... The second intituled The
English housewife: containing the inward and outward vertues which
ought to be in a compleate women: as her phisicke, cookery ... distillation, perfumes, ... brewing, baking, and all other things belonging to an
houshold* (London: R. Jackson, 1615), 73.

stir to combine.

Cover with a tea towel and let
stand in a cool place for four hours,
preferably overnight.

Take spoonfuls of the mixture
and roll into balls the size of a large
marble. Place on a baking tray lined
with parchment.

Bake in a hot oven (160°C/
320°F) for about 10-15 minutes
until set.

In other words, gin and gingerbread took
on many guises during its long existence from
a warming treat for the poor at popular cultural
events, a by-employment for young women, a cer-
emonial tradition, and even the title of a modern-
day historical novel, Elizabeth Jeffrey's 1989 book
Gin and Gingbread.

By the summer of 1738, it was reported
that 7,000 unlicenced sellers were convicted in
regular court and another 5,000 were penalised
by the Office of Excise.[275] This was a gross exag-

---

275.   Peter Clark, 'The "Mother Gin" Controversy in the Early
Eighteenth Century', *Transactions of the Royal Historical Society*,
38 (1988), 80.

geration since less than 1,300 retailers were fined by the Office of Excise between the years 1736 and 1740.[276] (Nothing like exaggerations in the media to stir up negative sentiments against spirits sales and consumption.) Chandlers—an old generic term for dealers in just about anything—also represented a large chunk of London's gin-sellers. One newspaper reported that setting up a chandler's shop required 'neither much money nor experience to set up [and] afford an easy means of relief to indigent people'.[277] (Think of the convenience shops that pepper the street corners of major cities around the world. You'll get the idea.)

The fifth 'gin act'—*An Act enforcing the Execution of an act, made in the Ninth Year of the present Majesty's Reign*—which was passed on 20 May 1738, reinforced the previous year's law, making it a felony to attack any informer and condone the citizen's arrest of unlicenced gin-sellers,

---

276. Peter Clark, 'The "Mother Gin" Controversy in the Early Eighteenth Century', *Transactions of the Royal Historical Society*, 38 (1988), 80

277. Peter Clark, 'The "Mother Gin" Controversy in the Early Eighteenth Century', *Transactions of the Royal Historical Society*, 38 (1988), 69.

acknowledging that many members of the city's constabulary refused to apprehend friends and neighbours who sold spirits as one of the few ways that the poor made money.[278] Excised spirits sales declined only slightly to 5,439,377 gallons while beer sales marginally declined to 132,709,788 gallons.[279] This figure does not, of course, account for the quantities of unexcised spirits.

Instead of imposing further restrictions on production and despite the need to raise funds for the War of Succession (1740-1748), Parliament passed the sixth 'gin act'—*An Act for repealing certain Duties on Spirituous Liquors, and on Licences for retailing the same, and for laying Duties on Spirituous Liquors, and on Licences to retail the said Liquors*—on 22 March 1743, which reduced the annual retail licence to 9s (about £54 today) and reduced the excise on spirits to 2s (about £54 today) per 36-gallon barrel.[280] This measure escalated excised spirits production even

---

278. 11 George II, c. 26.
279. TNA: T64/72, 22 and 25.
280. 16 George II, c. 8.

higher to 8,203,243 gallons rather than lower, while excised beer quantities remained relatively stable at 131,287,896 gallons.[281]

The seventh 'gin act'—*An Act for granting a Duty to His Majesty, to be paid by Distillers, upon Licences taken out by them for retailing Spirituous Liquors*—passed on 17 June 1747, ordered distillers who lived and worked within the London and Westminster city limits to obtain an annual licence for £5 (about £583 today). The number of licences issued to just one licence per business and could only be taken out if they also paid £20 (about £2,332 today) per year in Church and poor rates.[282] The act also forbade distillers from retailing their spirits in any place other than in 'his, her, or their own publick Shop and Shops only, and in no more than One Shop by virtue of any One Licence.'[283] The penalty for forfeiture was £10 (about £1,166 today). Whatsmore, customers were not allowed to tipple in a licenced distiller's

281.   TNA: T64/172, 22 and 25.

282.   20 George II, c. 39.

283.   20 George II, c. 39.

shop. As you can imagine, these limitations and licences reduced excised spirits production to 7,310,081 gallons and saw excised beer increase to 135,878,652 gallons.[284]

Although the eighth and final 'gin act' of the eighteenth century—*An Act for granting to his Majesty an additional Duty upon Spirituous Liquors, and upon Licences for retailing the same ; and for repealing the Act of the twentieth Year of His present Majesty's Reign, intituled, An Act for granting a Duty to His Majesty to be paid by Distillers upon Licences to be taken out by them for retailing Spirituous Liquors; and for the more effectually restraining the retailing of distilled Spirituous Liquors; and for allowing a Drawback upon the Exportation of British made Spirits; and that the Parish of Saint Mary le Bon, in the County of Middlesex, shall be under the Inspection of the Head Office of Excise.* (Also known as the Tippling Act)— was intended to reduce spirits production and sales when it was issued in 25 June 1751, production had already marginally declined to 7,049,821 gallons without the stimulus of legislation, while

---

284.   TNA: T64/172, 22 and 25.

excised beer production increased to 142,803,072 gallons.[285] The statute increased excise to 13.5s (about £90 today) per 36-gallon barrel for spirits and prohibited street sellers from plying their trade just as the Company's ordinance had done in 1639. However, this time, distillers were banned from retailing their own wares altogether. Unlike the Company's ordinance which prohibited sales to inns, taverns, alehouses, and victualling houses, the act prescribed annual retail licences costing £2 (about £233 today) to be acquired by taverns, inns, victualling houses, coffee houses, and ale houses.

During the years of the eight 'gin acts' from 1729 to 1751, spirits production only reached a high point amid the events surrounding the War of Austrian Succession (1740-1748), which coincided with the government's timely need for war funding. The excise on spirits was a convenient source of funding for England's military efforts. Beer, on the other hand, benefitted the most from the eight 'gin acts' when the exportation of spirits was encouraged in 1733 and when retailer licences

---

285.   24 George II, c. 40.

were limited to conventional drinking outlets in 1751. It meant beer was more available to consumers plus beer already had traditional outlets like alehouses and inns already secured. So let's ask again: Did the alleged eight 'gin acts' actually lead to the end of the Gin Craze? Take a look at this table of the quantities of excised low wines that were distilled from molasses, cider, and malted grain in the years in which those 'gin acts' were set in motion as well as the 'strong waters' that were produced (Table 1):

Table 1. Quantities of Low-Wines and Resulting Strong Waters Distilled during the 'Gin Acts' Years, 1729-1760.

Year	Low wines from Molasses (gallons)	Low wines from Cider (gallons)	Low wines from Malted Grain	'Strong Waters' produced (gallons)
1729	1,265,554	32,074	6,461,544	4,708,774
1733	1,325,046	14,174	6,057,153	4,821,434
1736	1,495,814	74,621	8,476,004	6,116,314
1737	932,199	40,165	6,018,592	4,250,198
1738	1,028,425	86,084	7,261,010	5,439,337
1743	920,494	99,151	12,498,850	8,203,203
1747	423,740	111,524	11,367,536	7,310,081

Year	Low wines from Molasses (gallons)	Low wines from Cider (gallons)	Low wines from Malted Grain	'Strong Waters' produced (gallons)
1751	406,537	30,964	11,282,653	7,049,821
1757	256,192	949	5,231,625	3,714,810
1758	2,601,023	50,369	63,837	1,850,271
1759	2,477,360	301,227	29,615	1,829,134
1760	2,243,603	69,204	56,777	3,115,138

Source: TNA: T64/172, 25 and 26.

Don't forget, Wilson concluded that because of the bad grain harvests of the 1750s, Parliament was forced to periodically ban distillation in England altogether.[286] However, her deduction is invalidated by the Treasury's excise reports, which show that spirits production plummeted from 3,714,810 gallons in 1757 to a low of 1,829,134 gallons in 1759 before rising again to 3,115,138 gallons in 1760.[287] So although there was a decline in production quantities, spirits were still produced and excised. Wilson's conclusion is also rendered invalid by historian W.G. Hoskins's report that

286.   Constance Anne Wilson, *Water of Life: A History of Wine-Distilling and Spirits 500 BC to AD 2000* (Totnes, Devon: Prospect Books, 2006), 226.

287.   TNA: T64/172, 25.

between 1750 and 1759, England experienced only two deficit grain harvests and four good harvests, which would not necessitate a ban on grain distillation.[288] So, without a statute to back up her claim, it seems probable that there was never a complete ban on distillation. More than likely, severe restrictions were imposed on the grain purchases made by distillers. However, because beer was treated as a vital foodstuff, brewers did not experience any declines in production during the 1750s despite the two bad grain harvests. From the 133,347,708 gallons of beer produced in 1757, the quantity rose to 141,642,072 gallons in 1758, increasing again to 150,590,016 gallons in 1759 and again to 158,020,776 gallons in 1760.[289] While John Chartres made an interesting point about war as well as embargoes on foreign imports and exports stimulating the Gin Craze, England's continued involvement in foreign wars beyond

---

288.   W.G. Hoskins, 'Harvest Fluctuations and English Economic History, 1620-1759', *The Agricultural History Review*, 16/1 (1968), 15-31.

289.   W.G. Hoskins, 'Harvest Fluctuations and English Economic History, 1620-1759', *The Agricultural History Review*, 16/1 (1968), 22.

1757 does not explain the end of the Gin Craze. Historian Peter Clark comes closer to developing a plausible cause for this societal change. He postulated that advancements in brewing contributed to ending the Gin Craze and stimulated a revival in beer consumption. This event, he attributed in part, to the invention of porter and other stout beers coupled with the establishment of the tied house networks by large-scale brewers, plus the technological advances in malting, hops drying, and brewing.[290] For example, nineteenth-century English brewer Henry Stopes documented eight patents granted between 1634 and 1660 that were dedicated to improving the quality and output of the malting process and brewing techniques.[291] Other patents enhanced bottling processes and boiling copper designs (a 'copper' was a large vessel used for heating liquids, washing dishes and

---

290.   Peter Clark, *The English Alehouse: A Social History 1200-1830* (Burnt Mill: Longman Group, 1983), 83; Peter Clark, 'The "Mother Gin" Controversy in the Early Eighteenth Century', *Transactions of the Royal Historical Society,* 38 (1988), 83.

291.   Henry Stopes, *Malt and Malting: An Historical and scientific and Practical Treatise, Showing as Clearly as Existing Knowledge Permits What Malt Is and How to Make It* (London: Lyon, 1885), 468.

clothing, and for brewing), contributing even more to the common brewing trade's evolution.[292]

   While geneva is villified as the unregulated and occasionally outright lethal spirit of the Gin Craze in the existing history books, eighteenth-century distillation manuals suggest that commercial distillers—both regulated and unregulated—produced some form of juniper-forward spirit of respectable quality that was sold as geneva. For example, eighteenth-century distiller and advice manual author George Smith offered up three recipes that compared cost of goods sold with potential sales prices:[293]

Royal Geneva	l	s	d
30 gallons of proof Malt-spirits at 18 d.	02	05	00
7 pounds of Juniper-berries at 3d.	00	01	09
Coals, and working	00	01	00
	02	07	09
For sale	l	s	d
30 gallons of Royal Geneva at 2 s. 4d.	03	10	00

---

292.   Henry Stopes, *Malt and Malting: An Historical and scientific and Practical Treatise, Showing as Clearly as Existing Knowledge Permits What Malt Is and How to Make It* (London: Lyon, 1885), 468..

293.   George Smith, *A Compleat Body of Distilling, Explaining the Mysteries of that Science in a most easy and familiar Manner* (London: Henry Lintot, 1738), 49.

Best Geneva	l	s	d
30 gallons of proof Malt-spirits at 18 d.	02	05	00
8 lbs of Juniper-berries at 3d.	00	02	00
Coals, and working	00	01	00
	02	08	00
For sale	l	s	d
35 gallons of Royal Geneva at 2 s.	03	10	00

Geneva	l	s	d
30 gallons of proof Malt-spirits at 18 d.	02	05	00
10 lbs of Juniper-berries at 3d.	00	02	06
Coals, and working	00	01	00
	02	08	06
For sale	l	s	d
45 gallons of Geneva at 20d.	03	15	00

What is intriguing about Smith's recipes is that they offered products that appealed to three different economic levels of consumer. This suggests that his readership of commercial distillers no longer catered to only the gentry or the poor—in extremes. He suggested in his book that commercial distilling had settled into a pre-industrial model that could accommodate larger-scale production with a conscious eye toward profitability. In other words, Smith's musings about eighteenth-century geneva demonstrate that not all distillers compounded genevas as Defoe and other journalists of the time would have people believe. As he noted:

> Geneva hath more several and different names and titles, than any other liquor that is sold here: as double Geneva, royal Geneva, celestial Geneva, Tittery, Collonia, Strike-fire, &c. and gain'd such universal applause, especially with the common people, that by moderate computation, there is more of it in quantity sold daily in a great many Distillers shops, than of Beer and Ale vended in most publick houses, with this farther advantage, that Geneva is saleable the next day after its being distill'd, which is not to be practiced in the others:[294]

However, Smith did go on to say that geneva made by any of these recipes 'wonderfully improves by keeping, especially when it is full

---

294.   George Smith, *A Compleat Body of Distilling, Explaining the Mysteries of that Science in a most easy and familiar Manner* (London: Henry Lintot, 1738), 49-50.

proof' which some distillers lay their goods 'for eight or nine months', resulting in a mellowed a commodity sold for twice the price and 'preferable to other liquors of dearer prices.[295] In other words, barrel-aged geneva tasted better than it did straight from the still.

Geneva manufacture took another turn at the end of the Gin Craze, when Osmond Cooke filed Patent #660 on 2 February 1751 recipe that more closely resembled an English *aqua vitæ* or *aqua fructum* style of spirit, employing additional botanicals other than juniper berries, plus sweetening and colouring:

> A new method of cleansing and improving British Spirits to make greater perfection...equal in every respect to the best Holland or Cologne Geneva. Take 300 gallons spirits, 12 lb raisin stalks, 12 lb. of sandiver [which appears to be glass galls], 3 hands of laurel, 4 lb bitter almonds, 150 lb juniper berries, 4

---

295. George Smith, *A Compleat Body of Distilling, Explaining the Mysteries of that Science in a most easy and familiar Manner* (London: Henry Lintot, 1738), 50.

lb saltpetre and red argol calcined,
dulcify with 56 lb sugar; tincture
with an infusion of prunes and burnt
sugar.[296]

There was another feature of the post-Gin
Craze decades that bears mentioning here: the
rise of the 'gentleman distiller'. This shouldn't
come as a complete surprise since Parliament
passed more and more laws that made distilling too expensive for any but the wealthiest Brits.
A few members of the gentry joined the distilling trade at this time. Most notable of these was
John Booth who moved from Lincolnshire to London, setting up a successful distillery and brand—
Booth's Gin—by 1740.[297] His son Philip as well as
his grandsons William, John Gillyat, and Felix
followed in his footsteps, operating their business
out of 55 Turnmill Street in London's Clerkenwell
district. The reasons why gentlemen distillers

---

296.   Frederic Arthur Filby, *A History of Food Adulteration and
Analysis* (London: G. Allen & Unwin Limited, 1934), 159.

297.   There is a discrepancy in Booth's location, because Parliamentary records say both John's and William's distilleries were
situated in Stanstead from 1790 through 1818 when William Booth's
offices were registered in Brentford.

gained prominence in the nineteenth-century gin trade becomes apparent when you think about how much the cost of doing business escalated because of rising taxation, licencing, technological advancements, and new inventions, which are the subject of the next chapter.

The Gin-Shop as depicted by George Cruikshank in Charles Dickens' Sketches by Boz, 1839 (Source: private collection).

CHAPTER SEVEN

'...BY means of the Hydrometer'[298]

The invention of Sikes's hydrometer and the column still in the 1800s caused a great leap forward in the quality of distilled spirits, which sparked a resurgence of consumer passion for spirits, and brought with it coffee houses, oyster bars and all sorts of other new drinking establishments.

I N THE SAME WAY that English beer experienced a revival thanks to the invention of new beer styles plus technological advancements in malting, hopping, and yeast cultivation, so did the distillation of English gin. Five stages ushered in the next phase in this evolution: the lead up to

---

298.   Frederic Arthur Filby, *A History of Food Adulteration and Analysis* (London: G. Allen & Unwin Limited, 1934), 160.

the development of the spirit called 'London gin'. First, Parliament took another approach to tempering English drinking culture when it passed *An Act to Encourage the Consumption of Beer*e on 8 July 1823 which was intended to lower the consumer pricing of beer by reducing the excise on beer to 5s (about £14.36 today) per 36-gallon barrel. Porter and other strong beers were excised at double the rate at 10s (about £28.72 today) per 36-gallon barrel.[299] But did it really rekindle beer drinking and dampen spirits sipping? We think not. Excise officers reported that in London alone 5,398,080 gallons of rectified spirits (meaning: licensed gin) were distilled between 6 January 1821 and 5 January 1822 and 5,872,009 gallons between 6 Janaury 1822 and 5 January 1823.[300] And that's not taking into consideration how much was manufactured elsewhere in England.

The second stage has been lightly touch upon in the history books. But there was a lot more

---

299.   4 George IV, c. 51.

300.   House of Commons, 'ACCOUNTS relating to British Spirits, Raw and Rectified, in each Excise Collection in England, in the Stocks of Rectifiers, 1821-1823', 21 June 1824.

to the 153 clauses or paragraphs that comprised *An Act to repeal the Duties payable in respect of Spirits distilled in England, and of Licences for distilling, rectifying or compounding such Spirit, and the Sale of Spirits; and to impost other Duties in lieu thereof; and to provide other Regulations for the Collection of the said Duties, and for the Sale of Spirits, and for the Warehousing of such Spirits, without Payment of Duty, for Exportation* which was passed on 27 June 1825 that changed the course of the distilling trade more than any of the supposed eight 'gin acts' ever could.[301] Here are the highlights:

Paragraph II set excise rates on 'Spirit of the Strength of Hydrometer Proof' at £35 (about £2,010 today) per 100 gallons—or 0.0003p (about 0.001p today) per dram. It's a figure that barely affected the end price of spirits to consumers. This charge was less than half what it had been in 1690 when the excise was 0.0049d (about 0.25p today) per dram. For obvious reasons, while this rate was intended to thwart the smuggling of foreign spir-

---

301.   6 George IV c. 80.

its, it did nothing to discourage the consumption of domestic spirits on home shores.[302]

Paragraph III compelled the licencing of distillers at £10 (about £575 today) per year; rectifiers at £10 (about £575 today) per year; spirits dealers who were not retailers at £10 (about £575 today) per year; and spirits retailers at £10 (about £575 today) per year. This may not seem like much unless you think about the fact that before this law was enacted, there were distillers who manufactured base spirits and rectified the same spirits. This cost them £20 (about £1,150 today) per year in licences. If that same distiller also had a retail shop on premises, another £10 (about £575 today) annual licence tagged on a third cost to production. For most English distillers, it was far more practical to stick to one form of production and think twice about retailing from the same premises.

---

302.   James Nicholls, 'Drinking Cultures and Consumption in England: Historical Trends and Policy Implications', *Memorandum* AL 59 (2009) <https://publications.parliament.uk/> [accessed 15 June 2022].

Paragraph IX of the statute stated that the space in which a distillery was located had to be inhabited by a 'Householder, occupying a Tenement or tenements of the yearly Value of Twenty Pounds [about £1,148 today] or upwards, and for which he, she or they shall be accordingly assessed in this own Name, … and shall also pay to the Parish Rates…'. [303] This meant only responsible people who could afford to pay a sizeable rent and place their own name on a lease were allowed to distil spirits. The next clause set two of the most serious limitations on distillery size and type.

Paragraph X prohibited any English distiller from owning a still with a capacity of less than 400 gallons (18 hectolitres). From that day onward, only large-scale, commercial distilleries operated by licenced distillers could produce spirits. This cut out most of London's distillers, paring it down to the Company's member-distillers and the city's gentlemen distillers. [304] (In practice, this statute remains unchanged today. As of Septem-

---

303.   6 George IV c. 80.

304.   6 George IV c. 80.

ber 2020, the HMRC retains the power to refuse a licence to any distillery in which the largest still is 18 hectoliters or less. For this reason, only provisional licences are granted to craft distilleries in Great Britain.)

Paragraph XXXVI prohibited anyone who made beer, sweets, vinegar, cider, perry, or refined sugar from distilling, rectifying, or compounding spirits on the same premises.[305] The penalty for committing this offence was a sizeable £200 (about £11,486 today) fine for each incident. There was no way to diversify a distilling business model after that. (This one especially hit the rum distilling business in England hard. Yes there was one at the time.

Next, three clauses in this statute set out to control the actual manufacturing processes used to make spirits. Paragraph XLV ordered distillers who intended to manufacture spirits with sugar or potatoes to notify the Office of Excise or face a similar £200 (about £11,486 today) penalty per

---

305.   6 George IV c. 80.

incident.[306] Paragraph LVII stipulated that a distiller who wished to make and use 'bub'—a blend of meal and yeast—that was added to warm wort to encourage speedier fermentation had to give:

> Notice in Writing to the proper Officer surveying the Distillery of such Distiller, specifying the Time when, and the particular Vessel or Vessels in which such Companion is to be made or prepared, and the particular Wash, fermenting Back or Backs into which the same is to be put, and also specifying the Quantity of such Composition to be put in every such Back, which Quantity shall not exceed the Proportion of Five Gallons for every One Hundred Gallons of the Wort or Wash to which such Composition is to be added.

If a distiller failed to follow this rule, a £200 (about £11,486 today) penalty was issued per incident. Paragraph LXX made it illegal to blend sugar, syrup, 'or any glutinous or saccharine' or other

---

306.   6 George IV c. 80.

sweet substances into 'into Low Wines, Feints or Spirits' to affect the 'Strength thereof respectively being ascertained by the hydrometer'.[307] Doing so meant the liquid was seized and the distiller fined a £200 (about £11,486 today) penalty per incident. Basically, these three clauses cautioned distillers against making any alterations or adulterations to distillation that weren't already sanctioned by Parliament and consequently by the Office of Excise who reported these sorts of misdeeds that ended up being placed into law.

Despite the fairly frequent calls to ban the street-selling of spirits, Paragraphs CXXXVIII, CXL, CXLI, and CXLII reiterated one more time for the hard of thinking that hawking, selling, or 'exposing to Sale' any spirits 'in or about the Streets, Highways or other Placed, or in or from any Boat or other Vessel upon the Water, or in any other Manner or Place whatsoever' except for those that were previously authorised such as distiller's shops, alehouses, inns, and taverns.[308]

---

307.   6 George IV c. 80.

308.   6 George IV c. 80.

If caught, the seller had his or her wares confiscated and that person was fined £100 (about £5,750 today) for each offence, which was enough to land any poor spirits seller in the workhouse in no time flat. How did they get caught? Informants. Any citizen—law abiding or not—could make a citizen's arrest and notify a 'Constable, Headborough, Tythingman, Churchwarden, Overseer of the Poor' or any other type of peace or parish officer. If the offender was later found guilty and was convicted, the person who made the arrest could receive a reward of up to £50 (about £2,880 today) for each case they brought to justice. The big 'however' was that if an offender snitched on another offender, the informant could be acquitted of guilt and any penalty. In the end, informants were not the most popular people in London. Consequently, not that many people made money by this insidious means.

The third stage toward a major evolution in gin-making saw two statutes passed within a month of each other that tipped the scales in favour of beer, ale, and cider—an important domestically-produced inebriant in the West Country.

An Act to repeal certain of the Duties on Cyder in the United Kingdom, and on Beer and Ale in Great Britain was passed on 16 July 1830, which ended the excise charged on beer, ale, and cider.[309] (Yes, it took a long time from the passage of the Cider Act—*An Act to explain and amend such Part of an Act made in the last Session of Parliament (intituled, "An Act for granting to His Majesty several additional Duties upon Wines imported into this Kingdom; and certain Duties upon all Cyder and Perry; ; and for raising the Sum of Three Millions Five Hundred Thousand Pounds, by Way of Annuities and Lotteries, to be charged on the said Duties") as relates to Cyder and Perry made in this Kingdom* —that was passed on 27 March 1764 to really take hold in England.[310] (But then cider and perry were regional drinks in a part of the country that was filled with emotionally charged English apple and pear growers—the West Country.) Next, *An Act to permit the general Sale of Beer and Cyder by Retail in England*— commonly known as the Beerhouse Act—was passed a week later, on 23 July 1830.

---

309.   11 George IV and William IV, c. 51.

310.   4 George III, c.7.

The statute was intended to encourage consumers to drink beer instead of spirits by enabling anyone who was willing to pay the excise on beer as well as purchase an annual seller's licence for £2 2s (about £142 today) could retail beer, ale, and cider.[311] (That was about £8 cheaper than the licence for selling spirits.) And brewers were finally relieved of the excise burden. Restrictions on the venues that could retail beer, ale, and cider were lifted in favour of encouraging the opening of more beer houses. As historian James Nicholls noted, 'within one year 24,000 beer shops had opened, rising to 40,000 within three years' but 'annual per capita consumption of beer, however, fell over the next three years before rising from 1834' until the act was amended that year and eventually repealed in 1869.[312] The relaxation of regulations on brewing as an attempt to discourage distilling only encour-

311.   11 George IV & William IV, c.62.

312.   James Nicholls, 'Drinking Cultures and Consumption in England: Historical Trends and Policy Implications', *Memorandum* AL 59 (2009) <https://publications.parliament.uk/> [accessed 15 June 2022]. 59.

aged the continued manufacture of lower-quality spirits that appealed to the poor.

That's right. The adulteration of spirits continued throughout the early nineteenth century. German chemist Frederick Accum was not enamoured with English malt spirit, so he encouraged adulteration. He wrote in his 1820 book *A Treatise of Adulterations of Food and Culinary Poisons* that:

> MALT spirit, or gin, the favourite liquor of the lower order of people, which is characterized by the peculiar flavour of juniper berries, over which the raw spirit is distilled, is usually obtained from a mixture of malt and barley: sometimes both molasses and corn are employed, particularly if there be a scarcity of grain.

Frederick Accum went on to note that:

> If we examine gin, as retailed, we shall soon be convinced that it is a custom, pretty prevalent amongst dealers, to weaken this liquor considerably with water, and to sweeten

it with sugar. This fraud may readily be detected by evaporating a quantity of the liquor in a table-spoon over a candle, to dryness; the sugar will thus be rendered obvious, in the form of a gum-like substance when the spirit is volatilised.[313]

According to his research, fraudulent retailers purchased wholesale stocks of 'genuine gin' and blended it 8 parts spirit to 1 part water and 4 parts sugar. This adulteration does suggest that a sweetened gin such as an Old Tom might have had its start as an adulteration of 'genuine gin' rather than as a 'Sweet' which was the authorised spirit produced by the Company's member-distillers. There is no evidence that Old Tom gin existed prior to 1812, prior to a popular misconception that it was referenced in the 1755 book *The Life and Uncommon adventures of Captin Dudley Bradstreet,* because gin was poured through a tube that emerged from between a cast iron cat's paw for customers who had inserted a coin in the

---

313.   Frederick Accum, *A Treatise of Adulterations of Food and Culinary Poisons* (London: Longman, Rees, Hurst, Orme, and Brown, 1820), 265-266.

cat's mouth. (This somehow became a myth of Old Tom's origins, although at the time it was known as 'puss and mew.') Further research by historians could yield a more definitive origin to Old Tom gin from either a legitimate or adulterated source.

Returning to Accum's diluted and sweetened adulteration, there was a flaw in its manufacture. Juniper berries and anise tend to louche when the oils meet with too much water: the diluted gin appears cloudy. Occasionally, retailers attempted to clear their product by adding a blend of alum and water which was allowed to rest for 24 hours.[314] Other less reputable retailers used a poisonous mixture of sulphate of lead and alum solutions to clarify the louched liquid. Once it was fined or cleared, it was sweetened with additional sugar and given a 'false strength' with the addition of grains of paradise, Guinea pepper, capsicum, and 'other acrid and aromatic substances.'[315]

---

314.   Frederick Accum, *A Treatise of Adulterations of Food and Culinary Poisons* (London: Longman, Rees, Hurst, Orme, and Brown, 1820), 266-267.

315.   Frederick Accum, *A Treatise of Adulterations of Food and Culinary Poisons* (London: Longman, Rees, Hurst, Orme, and Brown, 1820), 271-272.

How could excise men or other officials determine that a stock of gin or any other spirit had been diluted by a nefarious distiller or retailer? This was an important question not only for consumers, but for the importers and exporters of spirits as well as for the ever-watchful Office of Excise.

The fourth stage in this major gin-making evolution was when Sikes's hydrometer came into widespread use as the standard and official means of determining the specific gravity of liquor. Historian Frederick Arthur Filby in his 1934 study of food adulteration deduced that during the eighteenth century there was one 'very widespread practice, namely, that of watering down spirits.'[316] Techniques for detecting this disreputable behaviour were reported by eighteenth-century German chemist Caspar Neumann who found four methods that were commonly used to determine the strength of spirits including:

316.   Frederic Arthur Filby, *A History of Food Adulteration and Analysis* (London: G. Allen & Unwin Limited, 1934), 160.

Table of specific gravities by Sykes' hydrometer,

Temperature, 60°

60	70		80		90		100		110	
S. G.	Wt.	S. G.	Wt.	S. G.	Wt.	S. G.	Wt.	S. G.	Wt.	S. G.
922	70	942	80	961	90	981	100	1000	110	1020
924	1	943	1	963	1	983	1	1002	1	1022
926	2	945	2	965	2	985	2	1004	2	1024
928	3	947	3	967	3	987	3	1006	3	1026
930	4	949	4	969	4	989	4	1008	4	1029
932	5	951	5	971	5	991	5	1010	5	1031
934	6	953	6	973	6	993	6	1012	6	1033
936	7	955	7	975	7	995	7	1014	7	1035
938	8	957	8	977	8	997	8	1016	8	1037
940	9	959	9	979	9	999	9	1018	9	1039

Alcoholometric table for use with a hydrometer as seen in Muspratt's Chemistry (Source: private collection).

1. On shaking a little [spirit] in a phial a number of bubbles arise upon the surface; the more numerous the bubbles and the more quickly they disappear, the more spirituous is the liquor.

2. If some of the spirit be poured upon Oil of Olive or Oil of Almonds, the oil arises to the surface more or less hastily according as the liquor contains more or less

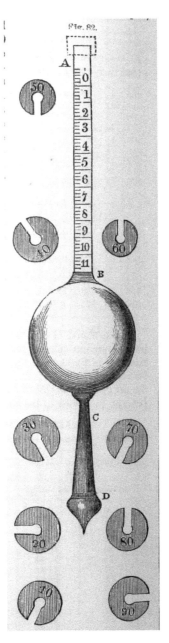

Sikes's Hydrometer as seen in Musptratt's Chemistry *(Source: private collection).*

phlegm. In pure spirit it does not rise at all.

3. By means of the hydrometer [of which more later].

4. Some set the brandy on fire, and judge of its strength by the quantity of phlegm or water that remains after the burning; such as leaves half its quantity is held to be of sufficient strength for brandy, and called Proof. The Phlegm thus freed from the spirituous part will readily discover by its taste how much or how little the brandy participated of nauseous matter.[317]

The oil test mentioned by Neumann was one of the oldest of methods for testing spirit strength, dating from the fifteenth century.[318] However, importers and distillers relied more upon the 'bead', 'crown' or 'proof vial' test up until

---

317.   Caspar Neumann, *The Chemical Works of Caspar Neumann, M.D. Abridged and Methodized with Large Addition, Second Edition, Volume II* (London: J. and F. Rivington, 1773), 258-259.

318.   William J. Ashworth, *Customs and Excise: Trade, Production, and Consumption in England, 1640-1845* (Oxford: Oxford University Press, 2003), 264.

the early eighteenth century.[319] Historian William J. Ashworth noted that the 'expansion and importance of the spirit duties made such methods [as these] appear too arbitrary', resulting in frequent clashes of opinion amongst distillers, merchants, and, of course, excise officers.[320] The proposed solution to this problem was the 'proof spirit' method, which involved weighing half rainwater or distilled water and half spirit and setting the result against a standard measure of specific gravity—or the density of the spirit divided by the density of water.[321] For example, proof spirit weighed 7 lb 12 oz per gallon with a specific gravity of 0.923 at the temperature of 51° Fahrenheit. If a distillate was 25 per cent over proof, 25 gallons of water

319.   William J. Ashworth, *Customs and Excise: Trade, Production, and Consumption in England, 1640-1845* (Oxford: Oxford University Press, 2003), 265.

320.   William J. Ashworth, *Customs and Excise: Trade, Production, and Consumption in England, 1640-1845* (Oxford: Oxford University Press, 2003), 265.

321.   William J. Ashworth, *Customs and Excise: Trade, Production, and Consumption in England, 1640-1845* (Oxford: Oxford University Press, 2003),265.

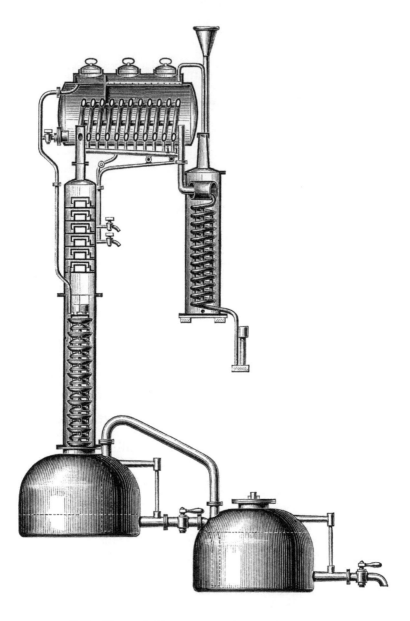

Cellier-Blumenthal's continuous column still
(Source: Alamy).

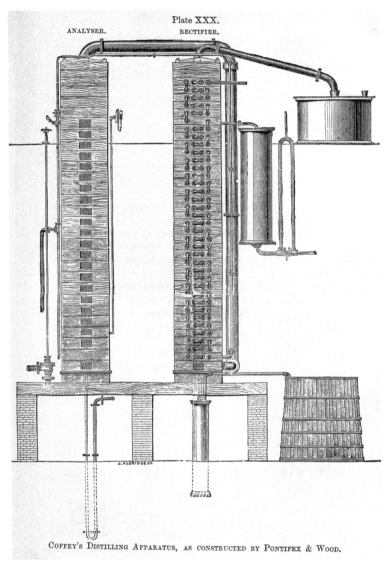

The Coffey still (Source: Science Photo Library).

were needed to reduce 100 gallons of distillate to 'proof spirit' strength.[322]

Another way to determine the strength of spirits was by densimetry, using a hydrostatic balance that was based on the ancient Greek mathematician Archimedes' principle. Using a pyncnometer, the volume and density of a liquid was measured by immersing a cyclinder in the liquid and measuring the vertical upward thrust from the liquid equal to the weight or gravity of the displaced liquid. This was equally inefficient at providing an accurate confirmation of alcohol content in a test liquid.

The flotation system offered the most plausible way for excise officers, distillers, and retailers to check spirit strength. One flotation device—the hydrometer—was invented by London engine maker John Clarke, in 1725, upon the request of a local distillery. In the *Philosophical Transactions of the Royal Society* of 1725, Clarke claimed his instrument would:

---

322.   William J. Ashworth, *Customs and Excise: Trade, Production, and Consumption in England, 1640-1845* (Oxford: Oxford University Press, 2003), 265.

>...acertain the true strength of
>proof of Brandy, rum, malt or molas-
>ses spirits, without tasting the same,
>or trusting to the uncertainty or fal-
>lacy of the proof vial.[323]

Taking cues from earlier flotation devices such as the glass bulb method designed by Robert Boyle in 1669, Clarke's design employed a series of weights that more efficiently calibrated the measurement. His work was officially sanctioned by the Royal Society in 1730 and was widely adopted by excise officers, but only gradually implemented by 'reluctant distillers and merchants.'[324]

There was a caveat to employing this device. Frederic Accum noted that:

>...as the difference of temperature
>affects materially the specific gravity
>of spirituous liquors, a thermom-
>eter, and tables of the concentration
>of strength [alcoholometric tables]

---

323.   William J. Ashworth, *Customs and Excise: Trade, Production, and Consumption in England, 1640-1845* (Oxford: Oxford University Press, 2003), 266.

324.   William J. Ashworth, *Customs and Excise: Trade, Production, and Consumption in England, 1640-1845* (Oxford: Oxford University Press, 2003), 267.

as denoted by the hydrometer, are used in the application of the instrument. The officer of the Excise has therefore only to turn to the tables opposite the indication, and immediately under the temperature he finds the percentage of the strength of the liquor.[325]

It is interesting to note that Clarke's device was never patented nor did it appear in any statutes passed by Parliament that were related to revenue and taxation until 21 January 1762 when *An act for more effectually preventing the excessive use of spirituous liquors for home consumption by laying additional Duties upon Spirits made in Great Britain or imported into the same; and for better regulating and encouraging the Exportation of British-made Spirits; and for securing the Payment of the Duties upon Spirituous Liquors* decreed that a standard gal-

---

325.   Frederick Accum, *A Treatise of Adulterations of Food and Culinary Poisons* (London: Longman, Rees, Hurst, Orme, and Brown, 1820), 252. In 1794, the Clerk of the Royal Society George Gilpin drafted tables of the specific gravity of liquor for every degree Fahrenheit from 30°F to 80°F, when compared with water at 60°F. The tables also the progression of 201 mixtures of alcohol to water from 100 parts alcohol with 0 parts water to 0 parts alcohol to 100 parts water. See Accum, 166.

lon of spirits should be composed of six parts by weight spirits and one part water for a total weight of 7 lb 13 oz at 51° Fahrenheit.[326] Clarke's hydrometer was finally legally sanctioned when *An act for making allowances to the dealers in foreign wines for the stock of certain foreign wines in their possession, at a certain time, upon which the duties on importation have been paid; and for amending several laws relative to the revenue of excise* was passed on 30 May 1787, decreeing that 'all spirits shall be deemed and taken to be of the degree of strength at which the said Hydrometer, called Clarke's Hydrometer, shall upon Trial by any Officer, or Officers of Excise, denote any such Spirits to be.'[327] Still, neither the inventors nor the government could leave well enough alone because excise officers, distillers, and retailers continued to contest the hydrometer-generated results.

The standard for the measurement of alcohol strength changed when on 23 May 1818, *An*

---

326.   William J. Ashworth, *Customs and Excise: Trade, Production, and Consumption in England, 1640-1845* (Oxford: Oxford University Press, 2003), 268; 2 George II, c.5.

327.   27 George III, c.31.

Act to repeal an Act made in the Fifty sixth Year of His present Majesty's Reign, for establishing the Use of an Hydrometer called Sikes's Hydrometer, in ascertaining the Strength of Spirits, instead of Clarke's Hydrometer; and for making other Provisions in lieu thereof, was passed. The change of heart was based simply on the way the two devices expressed the results. Clarke used minimal calibration. His hydrometer had three lines; one indicating proof, one indicating 10 per cent over proof, and one for 10 per cent under proof. Bartholomew Sikes had worked in excise for many years and was credited with solving many of the problems with Clarke's hydrometer before launching his own which was structurally very similar, but came more with accurate calibration and a book of alcoholometric tables for determining the proof of a spirit. Sadly, Sikes died in 1803 before he could obtain a contract from the Treasury to produce his device for use by the Office of Excise.[328] But thanks to the interventions of Sikes's daughter and her husband, instrument

---

328.   William J. Ashworth, *Customs and Excise: Trade, Production, and Consumption in England, 1640-1845* (Oxford: Oxford University Press, 2003), 276-278.

maker Robert Bate, as well as several high-profile court cases involving the deviation in results between the two instruments, Sikes's hydrometer prevailed. With the accuracy of determining strength stabilised amongst distillers, merchants, and excise officers, the quality level of English spirits (now called British spirits) took a step away from potential adulteration.

Finally, the fifth and final stage in the evolution of modern English gin-making arrived: the invention and adoption of the continuous column still. Able to sustain a constant process of distillation, this type of still behaves like a series of pot stills. Shaped in a vertical column fitted with plates that allowed the vapours to be progressively purified as they rise through the various stages, the column still significantly surpassed the ABV content achieved in a pot still. A few continuous-column still designs appeared in early nineteenth-century Europe, most notably the column still designed, in 1818, by French engineer J. B. Cellier-Blumenthal.[329]

With the invention of the Coffey still (Patent #5974 which was granted on 5 February 1831) and the establishment of still makers Aeneas Coffey and Son in London, in 1835, a cleaner, purer grain spirit exponentially changed the flavour, aroma, and quantity of distillates produced in London. For example, as *aqua fructum* made in a continuous column still and subsequently rectified in a pot still no longer tasted like heavy, new-make whisky. Now, it had a distinctively crisper character than its seventeenth-century ancestor, simply because the base spirit made on the continuous column still had a more neutral profile. The redistillation of this spirit with botanicals in a pot still highlighted the volatiles extracted from the herbs, fruits, and spices without competing with the character of the malted barley, malted or unmalted wheat, or molasses. With this

---

329.   R. J. Forbes, *Short History of the Art of Distillation: From the Beginnings up to the Death of Cellier Blumenthal* (Leiden: Brill, 1948), 287-288 and 301.

last change, the style known as London dry gin emerged in the mid-1800s.

Interest in the Coffey still reached Parliament when it ordered the Office of Excise to collect details on the use of this design throughout England, Scotland, and Ireland.[330] The report that was generated only 16 years after its invention showed that Coffey's stills were quickly licenced for use in a few key distilling centres, including east and south London, Bristol, Bromley in Hertfordshire, Newcastle, Brentford and Wandsworth in Surrey, and Worcester.

Even though spirits drinking declined after 1751 as we mentioned earlier, historian Peter Clark noted that 'demand [for gin and other spirits] revived from the 1780s and unofficial retailing spread like wildfire'.[331] The Treasury's excise reports indicate that in 1803 excised spirits rose to 23,952,971 gallons over five times greater than the

---

330.   House of Commons, 'RETURN ' of Licensed Distillers in *England, Scotland*, and *Ireland*; specifying the Situation and Excise Collection in which such Distilleries are situate;...', 6 June 1851.

331.   Peter Clark, *The English Alehouse: A Social History 1200-1830* (Burnt Mill: Longman Group, 1983), 262.

George Cruikshank's 1820 illustration of a gin palace (Source: private collection).

4,868,996 gallons produced in 1753.[332] Parliament started tracking the output of key large-scale distillers beginning in the 1790s: from metropolitan London, there were John and William Booth, John Liptrap, William Johnson, and Gosse & Benwell; from Bristol, there was Michael Castle.[333] The gallons of 'corn wash' produced by these 'malt distill-

---

332.　Great Britain, *Accounts and Papers of the House of Commons: Miscellaneous session 23 January to 11 July 1821*, 321; TNA: T64/172, 25.

333.　Great Britain, *Accounts and Papers of the House of Commons: Miscellaneous session 23 January to 11 July 1821*, 321; TNA: T64/172, 25.

ers' (differentiating them from rum distillers and the like) in Table 2 (see pages 260-261) provides a small sampling of each operations' output as the gin revival took shape.

What makes this table worth staring at is that there are obvious peaks and troughs in production levels among these high-volume distillers. You can see when William Booth took over the family business from his brother John Gillyat Booth in 1793. (We talked about the Booth family earlier.) You can also see when and why Samuel John Liptrap's Whitechapel distillery was the third largest in London by 1819.[334] (Liptrap himself was Master of the Worshipful Company of Distillers in 1788 and again in 1815.[335]) While there is little known about either Goss & Co or Johnson & Co distillers, it is interesting to note that they both produced substantial quantities and then went out of business by 1799. The blanks in certain years are

---

334. Survey of London, 'Whitechapel Sports Centre, Durward Street' <https://surveyoflondon.org/map/feature/615/detail/> [accessed 21 January 2024].

335. Michael Berlin, *The Worshipful Company of Distillers: A Short History* (Chichester: Phillimore & Co. Ltd., 1996), 75.

Table 2. Grain wash output of six key large-scale English malt distillers, 1790-1820.

Year	Castle & Co. (Bristol)	John Booth (Stanstead)	William Booth (Stanstead)	Goss & Co. (Battersea)	Liptrap & Co. (London)	Johnson & Co. (London)
1790	--	1,227,430	--	--	1,676,030	2,637,705
1791	--	1,798,538	--	--	1,420,390	2,709,587
1792	--	1,149,519	--	6,228,667	1,270,210	2,618,728
1793	1,807,107	1,257,446	--	5,747,125	1,290,149	2,215,744
1794	1,261,953	--	1,157,502	6,629,465	1,482,149	2,369,550
1795	1,497,747	--	1,275,227	6,529,569	1,607,795	2,173,518
1796	--	--	74,706	406,291	128,416	113,279
1797	763,236	--	1,206,820	3,357,797	1,536,744	1,349,572
1798	1,078,503	--	926,937	6,066,031	1,388,429	1,215,431
1799	1,170,305	--	1,275,623	--	1,121,096	1,198,777
1800	1,678,851	--	1,195,494	--	1,719,984	--
1801	--	--	--	--	--	--
1802	916,426	--	981,560	--	941,155	--
1803	1,481,492	--	1,530,590	--	1,372,871	--
1804	1,312,788	--	1,208,805	--	373,462	--

Year						
1805	1,700,630	--	1,334,893	--	--	--
1806	1,604,396	--	1,296,404	--	787,599	--
1807	1,942,684	--	1,363,966	--	1,279,539	--
1808	2,330,778	--	1,287,068	--	1,691,027	--
1809	81,186	--	6,375	--	47,637	--
1810	--	--	--	--	--	--
1811	--	--	--	--	--	--
1812	986,271	--	858,600	--	1,055,639	--
1813	--	--	--	--	--	--
1814	1,836,963	--	1,493,292	--	1,301,558	--
1815	2,432,450	--	2,034,299	--	2,378,421	--
1816	1,980,758	--	2,053,172	--	1,811,420	--
1817	1,879,862	--	2,430,713	--	2,340,300	--
1818	1,932,250	--	60,197	--	2,317,807	--
1819	2,155,485	--	--	--	2,269,878	--
1820	1,938,460	--	408,925	--	1,967,534	--

Source: House of Commons, 'An Account of the Quantity of Corn Wash: Distilled and by whom, between 5th July 1789 and the 5th July 1820; distinguishing the Quantities distilled each Year,' 28 March 1821.

the result of government bans on corn distillation from 10 July 1795 to 1 February 1797 to conserve grain stores for the War of the First Coalition; from 8 December 1800 to 1 January 1802 to continue grain conservaton during the War of the Second Coalition; from 30 June 1808 to 31 December 1810 to hold stock for the Peninsular War; and from 8 February 1812 to 1 December 1813 to conserve grain for the War of 1812.[336]

But the reason we added Michael Castle's Castle & Co distillery in Bristol is because his numbers are a bit misleading and bear closer study. Castle didn't always distil grain spirits. He also made sugar spirits (Read: rum). In 1809, he only produced 81,186 gallons of grain wash, which resulted in 15,425 gallons of spirits; he also produced 2,271,853 gallons of sugar wash to make 477,089 gallons of sugar spirits.[337] The fact that he

---

336.   House of Commons, 'An Account of the Quantity of Corn Wash: Distilled and by whom, between 5th July 1789 and the 5th July 1820; distinguishing the Quantities distilled each Year,' 28 March 1821 (London: HMSO, 1822).

337.   House of Commons, 'A Return of the Distillers Names in England, Residences, and Counties situated in…', 26 June 1821 (London: HMSO, 1822).

was the largest producer of spirits outside of London between 1821 and 1823—beating out Plymouth and Manchester—makes him a worthy candidate for future study by historians.[338] Next, in 1813, Castle produced 1,983,112 gallons of sugar wash and 416,453 gallons of sugar spirits, but no grain spirits. He made up for this void in 1814, when he produced 1,493,292 gallons of grain wash and 283,725 gallons of grain spirit. These figures ran nose-to-nose with William Booth who in those same years manufactured 1,871,122 gallons of sugar wash and 392,935 gallons of sugar spirit in 1813 and 1,493,292 gallons of grain wash and 283,725 gallons of grain spirit. As you can see, the numbers can be deceiving in these Parliamentary reports. You may think business was slow or just downright bad, before reaching a conclusion you must find out if the distillery was producing something in addition to their stated product in trade, such as grain spirits.

---

338. House of Commons, 'ACCOUNTS relating to British Spirits, Raw and Rectified, in each Excise Collection in England, in the Stocks of Rectifiers: 1821-1823', 21 June 1824 (London: HMSO, 1824).

Spirits distilled or rectified from sugar and used to make gin was still a sore point amongst England's malt distillers. A letter was sent to The Right Honourable the Chancellor the Exchequer by 26 distillers: among them were William Booth and Michael Castle.[339] The letter's contents can be summed up as economics: sugar spirits were cheaper to manufacture than grain spirits, and the planters in the British North American colonies pushed hard to get their molasses used in England to supply the huge demand for spirits. But as the signers of this letter noted:

> It has been fully stated to you, that to permit West India Rum, or other colonial spirit, to be converted by the rectifiers into English Gin, is not only a novelty in itself, but is directly

---

339. The letter was signed by John Currie, Leonard Currie, H. Waymouth, John Currie, senior, William Leader, John Atlee, James Langdale, Samuel Jones Vachell, James Mure, Joseph Claypole, T.V. Cooke, B. Smith, O.H Smith, R. Carrington, R. Carrington, junior, William Booth, Thomas Smith, George Smith, Levi Ames, Thomas Castle, M.H. Castle, Thomas Harris, Samuel Bowtree, George Saville, and William Carrington. House of Commons, 'Copy of a LETTER to The Right Honourable the Chancellor of the Exchequer, from the Corn Distillers in England, respecting the conversion of Rum into Gin by the Rectifiers; dated 30th May 1825'.

opposed to the long established
policy of this country.

This letter does leave us to wonder how much rum was being sold to rectifiers to produce English gin. And it does leave us worry that amongst the many hundreds of London distillers how many of the small distillers did, in fact, rectify rum into gin because it was cheaper than purchasing grain spirits. Finally, it just leaves us to worry that if you didn't purchase higher-priced gin from the wealthier, large-scale rectifiers you were drinking something that brought the whole industry into embarrassment. But that's our own opinion.

So, despite the alleged 30-year hiatus in gin production (or not) after the end of the Gin Craze that is implied by some historians, spirits returned to the English drinking culture's repertoire like a stampede of horses. Besides authorised retailers such as public houses and traditional venues such as taverns and inns, there were 'small shopkeepers involved in retailing liquor, often without permits' which were joined in London by the new crop of coffee-houses and oyster rooms.

Coffee-houses got their start at Oxford. Seventeenth-century diarist John Evelyn recorded on 10 May 1637 while he was in Oxford that he observed fellow Balliol College student Nathaniel Conopios, preparing and drinking a particular morning beverage, stating that:

> He was the first I ever saw drink coffee; which custom came not into England till thirty years after.[340]

With this remark, Evelyn placed coffee drinking as a rarefied practice among individuals who imported it from the Levant until the earliest known English coffee-house—the Angel Coaching Inn—opened in 1650.[341] Wilson reminded us that 'Coffee remained expensive, for it was costly to import and within a few years was

---

340.   John Evelyn, *The Diary of John Evelyn, Vol. I*, ed. by William Bray (London: M Walter Bunne, 1901), 9.

341.   Iulia Costache, 'The first Jewish settlements in the United Kingdom', Museum of Oxford <https://museumofoxford.org/> [accessed 15 December 2023].

made liable to excise duty.'[342] Selling for 'no more than a penny a dish' in licenced coffee houses by 1663 in London and elsewhere, coffee drinking spread to the homes of the gentry who embraced the intoxicant as a morning beverage despite the high price tag in 1693 of 6s (about £36 today) per pound.[343] Although coffee-houses initially offered an alcohol-free environment, eighteenth-century proprietors sometimes found themselves sharing space with distiller's shops which meant they could inadvertently offer customers spirits without impacting either owner's licences. For example, Mrs. Martin who owned Martin's Coffee-House at Charing Cross, in 1732, let the lower floor of the establishment for £25 per year to a distiller named Mr. Capstick.[344] Even though oys-

342.   Constance Anne Wilson, *Water of Life: A History of Wine-Distilling and Spirits 500 BC to AD 2000* (Totnes, Devon: Prospect Books, 2006), 405.

343.   Glady Scott Thomson, *Life in a Noble Household, 1641-1700*, Bedford Historical Series, I, (London: Jonathan Cape, 1940), 168-169; Constance Anne Wilson, *Water of Life: A History of Wine-Distilling and Spirits 500 BC to AD 2000* (Totnes, Devon: Prospect Books, 2006), 408.

344.   Old Bailey Proceedings Online <https:/www.oldbaileyonelin.ord/> [accessed: 18 December 2023].

ters had been served as common tavern food for quite some time, the oyster bar or oyster house made its appearance in London toward the end of the eighteenth century when establishments like Rules opened in 1798 and James Pimm opened his first oyster bar near the Old Billingsgate Market in 1823. It became customary for oysters and shellfish to be accompanied by either stout or spirits-based punches and cups. (Hence, the reason why Pimm's created and commercialised his gin-based fruit cup or sling.)[345] The late mixologist Wayne Collins was asked to replicate Pimm's No. 1 Cup back in the early 2000s. This recipe was the result, effectively reproducing the recipe from scratch as Mr Pimm himself must have done for years:

GIN CUP
1.5 oz [45 ml] gin
1 oz [30 ml] Italian vermouth
0.5 oz [15 ml] triple sec
0.5 oz [15 ml] maraschino liqueur
2 dashes Angostura bitters

---

345. Anistatia Miller and Jared Brown, 'Pimm's Cup', *The Oxford Companion to Spirits & Cocktails* (Oxford: Oxford University Press, 2022), 539.

Combine all ingredients in a glass
over ice. Stir for 30 seconds.

Beginning in the 1820s, Peter Clark noted
that 'the orthodox drink trade was also challenged
by a new type of establishment, the larger, often
quite elaborate or showy gin palace.'[346] Novelist
Charles Dickens described, in 1836, the gin pal-
aces situated in London's west end around St Giles,
Holburn, Covent Garden, Clare Market, and Drury
Lane, most eloquently when he wrote in *Sketches
by Boz* that:

> The hum of many voices issues from
> that splendid gin-shop which forms
> the commencement of the two
> streets opposite; and the gay build-
> ing with the fantastically ornamented
> parapet, the illuminated clock, the
> plate-glass windows surrounded by
> stucco rosettes, and its profusion
> of gas-lights in richly-gilt burners, is
> perfectly dazzling when contrasted

---

346.   Peter Clark, *The English Alehouse: A Social History 1200-
1830* (Burnt Mill: Longman Group, 1983), 262.

with the darkness and dirt we have just left.[347]

This resurgence of spirits consumption by the public married well with the progress made in the industrialisation of the distilling trade as the association of the word 'gin' with several spirits styles that featured juniper berries hallmarked the nineteenth-century version of the English distilling trade.

New ways of serving gin arose such as Gin Twist, the Dog's Nose, and the Gin Cocktail in drinking establishments:

GIN TWIST
1.5 oz [45 ml] gin
juice of one lemon
1 to 2 tsp granulated sugar
Place ingredients in a toddy glass. Fill the glass with hot water. Stir to dissolve the sugar and serve.

DOG'S NOSE
1 oz [30 ml] gin
1 pint [570 ml] stout or porter

---

347. Charles Dickens, *Sketches by Boz* (London: Chapman, 1895), 136.

Drop a shot glass of the gin into a
pint glass filled with stout or porter.

GIN COCKTAIL
2 oa [60 ml] gin
1 tsp granulated sugar
2 dashes aromatic bitters
Place ingredients in a glass. Stir. Add
a splash of water.

Of course, we haven't forgotten Gin &
Tonic! We've devoted the Appendix to the clues
to its origin for you to peruse on your own.

Whichever way gin was served, it was
served with more than one style of gin. The bottom line about the types of gins that were produced by the late 1800s was best summarised by
temperance writer John William Kirton, who in
his 1879 book *Intoxicating Drinks: Their History &
Mystery* commented on the regionality of styles
and character of British gin. He quoted distiller
Charles Tovey, saying that:

> Taste in the flavour of Gin varies in
> different localties, and that which
> may be palatable in one county may
> be distilled in another. The flavour

approved of in London and the Midland Counties would be rejected in the West of England, especially in the neighbourhood of Barnstaple and Bideford, where almost plain spirit is preferred, while in Plymouth and Cornwall a coarse imitation of Hollands has its general admirers. One hiuse in particular in Plymouth has monopoly for a peculiar flavour of its Gin, which would be unpalatable to those accustomed to a spirit of a different character.[348]

Tovey's remarks sound like they were uttered today. Many of us tell our listeners and readers the same thing: Gin can be made to appeal to many palates in many places. So long as it contains juniper berries as the dominant botanical, it can be called gin.

The recipe that Kirton 'found to be most generally approved in the majority of counties in England, and which has its admirers in the colonies' was a three-step rectification which he also

---

348. John William Kirton, *Intoxicating Drinks: Their History & Mystery* (London: Ward, Lock & Co., 1879), 52.

quoted from Charles Tovey, who spent his childhood as a distiller's apprentice before becoming a distiller himself. (The recipe below will give you hint as to why his apprenticeship may have been long and hard.)[349]

> Charge the still with 1,000 gallons of grain spirit at proof; add 25 lbs grey and white salts, 63 lbs coriander seeds; run off 1,200 gallons of spirit, average srtength 40 overproof; reduce to meet the strength of your flavour. For flavour, charge with 474 gallons of clean spirit, 41 overproof.
>
> Ingredients as follow:—3 cwt. 3 qrs. 12 lbs. German juniper berries, 27 lbs bitter orangepeel, 13-1/2 lbs angelica root. Run off until it becomes milky, reduce to 28 underproof, and force it thus:
>
> —To 900 gallons add 1-1/2 lb of alum, 3/4 lb salt of tartar; put in the latter first. To flavour the coriander spirit and complete the Gin, 22-1/2 per cent is generally used. The faints [sic] of this flavour can be worked,

---

349.   John William Kirton, *Intoxicating Drinks: Their History & Mystery* (London: Ward, Lock & Co., 1879), 52.

and the whole of the produce added to the first working.

Plain or London Gin is made thus:—700 gallons of the second rectification, 70 lbs German juniper berries, 70 lbs coriander seeds, 3-1/2 lbs almond cake, 1-1/2 lb of angelica root, 6 lbs liquorice powder.[350]

While the steps to making Tovey's recipe are far more complicated than what is produced today, its proportions and profile rang more clearly of a modern-day gin style. It also serves as a good stepping stone to the many ways nineteenth-century British distillers made gin.

Research chemist James Sheridan Muspratt, in the first of his two-volume book titled *Chemistry* surveyed the types of distillates produced with the clean, higher-proof spirit produced in continuous column stills by England's new generation of large-scale, nineteenth-cen-

---

350. John William Kirton, *Intoxicating Drinks: Their History & Mystery* (London: Ward, Lock & Co., 1879), 52; Charles Tovey, British & Foreign Spirits: Their History, Manufacture, Properties, etc. ((London: Whittakerm & Co., 1864), 97-98.

tury commercial distilleries.[351] He prefaced his presentation of the new spirits by hinting at gin's unique role as an ethnic beverage, remarking that: 'British spirit is but little known in the form in which it leaves the distillery because it receives from the rectifier the exclusive property by which it is rendered a household word.'[352] Muspratt elaborated on this position by adding that British gin was 'for the most part, manufactured by the rectifiers of the low-wines of the Scotch and English spirit or whisky fabricators.'[353] In other words, Muspratt defined British spirit—or gin— as the rectification of a first-distillation, unaged whisky—or new make whisky distilled from malted grain—with botanicals produced by two types of distillers—one who distilled the base spirit and one who rectified the spirit into gin. Again, the

---

351. James Sheridan Muspratt, *Chemistry: Theoretical, Practical & Analytical as Applied to The Arts and Manufactures*, Vol. I (London, William Mackenzie, 1860), 98-102.

352. James Sheridan Muspratt, *Chemistry: Theoretical, Practical & Analytical as Applied to The Arts and Manufactures*, Vol. I (London, William Mackenzie, 1860), 98-99.

353. James Sheridan Muspratt, *Chemistry: Theoretical, Practical & Analytical as Applied to The Arts and Manufactures*, Vol. I (London, William Mackenzie, 1860), 101.

connection between beer made from malted barley and high-proof spirit made from malted barley make them very close cousins indeed.

In his chapter on alcohol, Muspratt included six gin recipes, which he compiled from the notebook of 'one of the most extensive and respectable distillery rectifiers in the kingdom.'[354] A notable difference between these recipes and the 'rules' standardised by the Worshipful Company of Distillers in 1639 is that none of these formulations contain sugar. Muspratt's recipe for British Gin rectified:

> Three hundred gallons of liquor and
> six hundred and fifty gallons of spirit
> from a previous rectification, to
> which are added
> 95 lbs German juniper berries,
> 95 lbs coriander seeds,
> 47 lbs crushed almond cake,
> 2 lbs angelica root, and
> 6 lbs liquorice powder.
> …bring it to twenty-two per cent

---

354.   James Sheridan Muspratt, *Chemistry: Theoretical, Practical & Analytical as Applied to The Arts and Manufactures*, Vol. I (London, William Mackenzie, 1860), 101.

under proof. Then the whole is
pumped in to store casks for use:
the result being one thousand one
hundred gallons.[355]

His Cordial Gin formula offered the rectifier the option of adding cardamom or liquorice
powder which meant the person could make a
gin with a pungent, aromatic character or with a
sweetened profile without the use of sugar, rectifying:

... seven hundred of the product of the second rectification—if
improved stills are used, the product
of the first distillation answers—and
mix it with the following ingredients:
70 lbs German juniper berries,
56 lbs coriander seeds,
5 lbs almond cake, crushed or
broken,
1-1/2 lb orris root, broken,
2-1/2 lbs angelica root, cut,
1/2 lb cardamom or, instead of this

355. James Sheridan Muspratt, *Chemistry: Theoretical, Practical &
Analytical as Applied to The Arts and Manufactures*, Vol. I (London,
William Mackenzie, 1860), 101.

> 6 lbs liquorice powder are some-
> times added.

> …Run down the gin from the
> store cask, and make up to strength
> required—seventeen to twenty-two
> under proof.[356]

In this recipe, Muspratt suggests that a double-distilled base spirit— 'the product of the second rectification'—from a pot still could be more efficiently replaced by a single distilled spirit produced on a continuous column still.

To echo an earlier question: Was the option in Muspratt's recipe to sweeten the Cordial Gin with liquorice—a throwback to the popular pref-erence for Sweets during the eighteenth century? It is a point that deserves further research in the future by historians.

A variation on this Cordial Gin rectified 1,950 gallons of spirit with the following:

> 100 lbs juniper berries,
> 70 lbs coriander seeds,

356.   James Sheridan Muspratt, *Chemistry: Theoretical, Practical & Analytical as Applied to The Arts and Manufactures*, Vol. I (London, William Mackenzie, 1860), 101.

2 lbs orris root,
1 lb angelica root,
2 lbs calamus roots,
1/2 lb cardamom seeds.
The operations being the same as
noted in the preceding.[357]

This version of Cordial Gin was a more compact formulation that relied more on the robust character of juniper berries and coriander than the accompanying botanical notes. Another point to highlight is that Muspratt does not specify German juniper berries in this formula.

Muspratt's next two recipes are more familiar to today's palate. The Plain or London Gin formula follows the same pattern as the British Gin recipe but reduces the amount of almond cake, rectifying:[358]

700 gallons of second rectification,
70 lbs German juniper berries,
70 lbs coriander seeds,

---

357. James Sheridan Muspratt, *Chemistry: Theoretical, Practical & Analytical as Applied to The Arts and Manufactures*, Vol. I (London, William Mackenzie, 1860), 101.

358. James Sheridan Muspratt, *Chemistry: Theoretical, Practical & Analytical as Applied to The Arts and Manufactures*, Vol. I (London, William Mackenzie, 1860), 101..

> 3 -1/2 lbs almond cake,
> 1 12 lb angelica root,
> 6 lbs liquorice powder.

It should be noted that in this recipe, Muspratt called for double-distilled spirit from a pot still instead of a single-distilled spirit from a continuous column still. Furthermore, this recipe rectified nearly the same botanicals found in today's recipe for Tanqueray gin. (Tanquerary contains no almond cake but is made with the four other botanicals lised above.) However, it does not bear as close a resemblance to the now-common formulation for London dry gin as does Muspratt's Fine Gin recipe.[359] This rectification called for:

> 960 gallons of spirit, hydrometer proof,
> 96 lbs German juniper berries,
> 6 lbs coriander seeds,
> 4 lbs grains of paradise,
> 4 lbs angelica root,
> 2 lbs orris root,
> 2 lbs calamus root,

---

359. James Sheridan Muspratt, *Chemistry: Theoretical, Practical & Analytical as Applied to The Arts and Manufactures*, Vol. I (London, William Mackenzie, 1860), 101..

2 lbs orange peel.
80 or 90 lbs of liquorice powder are
occasionally added to impart color
and sweetness. [360]

In this instance, Muspratt only calls for the base spirit to be of 'hydrometer proof' or 57.15 per cent alcohol by volume. (Even today, gin distillers commonly cut neutral spirit with water to around this strength prior to rectification.) Fine Gin harkens back to the recipe for *aqua fructum* mentioned earlier from the 1639 edition of *The Distiller of London* (see page 151) because it pairs citrus notes of orange peel and coriander seed, augmented by woody and peppery notes, finished with colour and sweetness.

The sixth and final gin recipe in Muspratt's chapter—West Country Gin—was mentioned as being used to make 'British hollands', rectifying:

…seven hundred gallons of the second rectification, and flavor with 14 lbs German berries

---

360.   James Sheridan Muspratt, *Chemistry: Theoretical, Practical & Analytical as Applied to The Arts and Manufactures*, Vol. I (London, William Mackenzie, 1860), 101.

1-1/2 lbs calamus root, cut, and
8 lbs sulphuric acid[361]

Certainly, Muspratt intended to prescribe German juniper berries in this recipe. Muspratt commented that: 'This gin is much used in Cornwall, and particularly in the Western counties of England; it is also used in making British hollands and in that case mixed with about five per cent Fine Gin (see page 280) reduced to twenty-two per cent under proof with liquor'. [362] This would mean the spirit was around 35 per cent ABV, a few degrees below the modern legal limit for a gin. His notation suggests that as late as the mid-nineteenth century—some semblance of hollands or geneva was still produced not only in public houses, but in commercial distilleries that contained toxic elements used to replicate the spirituous heat found in all alcohols and to accentuate the pine aroma familiarly associated with juniper berries.

---

361.   James Sheridan Muspratt, *Chemistry: Theoretical, Practical & Analytical as Applied to The Arts and Manufactures*, Vol. I (London, William Mackenzie, 1860), 101.

362.   James Sheridan Muspratt, *Chemistry: Theoretical, Practical & Analytical as Applied to The Arts and Manufactures*, Vol. I (London, William Mackenzie, 1860), 102.

By contrast, Muspratt's making of Dutch hollands harkens back to Peter Shaw's description of Dutch geneva (see page 135) and details the process more thoroughly:

> One hundred and twelve pounds barley malt, and two hundred and twenty-eight pounds of ryemeal, are mashed with four hundred and sixty gallons of water, at 162°Fahr.; after infusion has taken place, cold water is added to bring the strength to forty-five pounds per barrel, or spec. grav. 1.047, at which strength, after it has cooled to 80°Fahr. It is run into the fermenting tun. To the contents of the fermenting back, which is about five hundred gallons, half a gallon of good yeast is added, fermentation speedily sets in the temperature rises to about 90°, and the attenuation is complete in forty-eight hours. After attenuation of the wash, from twelve to fifteen pounds per barrel of saccharine matter remain undercomposed in the fermented liquor. The wash and grains are then introduced into the

still, and the whole of the low-wines distilled over; these are subjected to a second distillation, and the distillate after rectification is the famous *geneva.* A few juniper berries and sometimes hops are added in the rectification to impart to the spirit a peculiar terebinthine [turpentine] flavor.[363]

The first two items to bring to your attention in this recipe are the use of double the amount of ryemeal to barley malt and the miniscule quantity of juniper berries. Referencing what we said before, this detailed recipe for Dutch hollands—also called genever—is diametrically opposed to the nineteenth-century gin recipes seen here as the directions for making scotch whisky as opposed to American rye whiskey. Muspratt noted some 'peculiarities' in this recipe, 'namely, the imperfect attenuation of the wort, and the small amount

---

363.   James Sheridan Muspratt, *Chemistry: Theoretical, Practical & Analytical as Applied to The Arts and Manufactures*, Vol. I (London, William Mackenzie, 1860), 100.

of yeast employed in bringing it about.'[364] He compared this to the quantity of spirits obtained from English distillers in which was about double that achieved by their Dutch counterparts.[365] From this presentation, he concluded that the 'only liquor in this country which can bear any comparison with that of Holland, is perhaps the illicit product.[366] So, how was English geneva produced? Muspratt offered three examples for our analysis. The first recipe charged the still with:

> ...nine hundred and fifty gallons of
> second rectification, [adding]
> 84 lbs juniper berries,
> 112 lbs coriander seeds,
> 6 lbs cassia buds,
> 4 lbs angelica root,
> 6 lbs calamus root,

364.   James Sheridan Muspratt, *Chemistry: Theoretical, Practical & Analytical as Applied to The Arts and Manufactures*, Vol. I (London, William Mackenzie, 1860), 101.

365.   James Sheridan Muspratt, *Chemistry: Theoretical, Practical & Analytical as Applied to The Arts and Manufactures*, Vol. I (London, William Mackenzie, 1860), 101.

366.   James Sheridan Muspratt, *Chemistry: Theoretical, Practical & Analytical as Applied to The Arts and Manufactures*, Vol. I (London, William Mackenzie, 1860), 101.

6 lbs almond cake,
1/2 lb cardamom.[367]

How does this recipe even remotely compare with the Dutch hollands recipe? Aside from this obvious juniper-berry led design, this formulation has far more in common with gin than genever.

Similarly, a recipe for what Muspratt called Plain Geneva required fewer ingredients, rectifying:

...nine hundred and fifty gallons of
second rectification...
84 lb juniper berries,
84 lbs coriander seeds,
 2 lbs almond cake,
2 lbs orris root,
2 lbs calamus.[368]

The formulation also suffers from the same misleading fault. It is more akin to a sim-

---

367.   James Sheridan Muspratt, *Chemistry: Theoretical, Practical & Analytical as Applied to The Arts and Manufactures*, Vol. I (London, William Mackenzie, 1860), 102.

368.   James Sheridan Muspratt, *Chemistry: Theoretical, Practical & Analytical as Applied to The Arts and Manufactures*, Vol. I (London, William Mackenzie, 1860), 102.

plified gin recipe than one for genever. Muspratt commented that the next geneva recipe was 'one which is much esteemed', preparing the spirit with salts before adding the botanicals to the macera-tion as follows:

> Add to nine hundred and fifty gal-lons—
> 14 lbs grey salts, and
> 4 lbs white salts.
> The rectification to be conducted with the usual care. At the second operation, add—
> 168 lbs juniper berries,
> 74 lbs coriander seeds,
> 12 lbs almond cake,
> 8 lbs grains of paradise,
> 8 lbs angelica root,
> 1 lb cardamom,,
> 2 lbs calamus.[369]

Salt was used in distillation as far back as the Arab alchemists in their early studies. Salt does not change the boiling point of alcohol, but it slightly raises the boiling point of water, allow-

---

369. James Sheridan Muspratt, *Chemistry: Theoretical, Practical & Analytical as Applied to The Arts and Manufactures*, Vol. I (London, William Mackenzie, 1860), 102.

ing easier extraction of alcohol in distillation. In continuous column stills, it is sometimes added near the top of the still, and helps to bring it to a higher ABV and purer spirit as a result.

In the end, Muspratt's six gin recipes and four geneva recipes demonstrate that: First, any juniper-berry predominant spirit produced in England was called 'gin' by the mid-nineteenth century. Second, the terms Geneva and gin were interchangeable by this time. Third, the term 'hollands' was attributed to two distinctly different spirits—British or English hollands and Dutch hollands—which had nothing in common. Fourth and finally, Muspratt's Fine Gin recipe and the Worshipful Company of Distillers of London's *aqua fructum* recipe do provide us with compelling evidence that the naissance of complex, balanced juniper-berry dominant spirits in the seventeenth century changed over time to appeal to the shifting flavour preferences of an audience of conspicuous consumers in the eighteenth and then nineteenth centuries.

The production of these new flavour pro-
files were impacted by technological advancements in still design and the greater output of
spirits to meet a revived demand by consumers.

conclusion

ND SO ENDS OUR JOURNEY through a very revised history of gin—at least as far as we've managed to track it today. (Remember what Professor Barry Reay said, 'There is no last word in the writing of history.' With this book, we think we've proven why.) There's more to research and write: Throughout this book, we suggested a few places for aspiring and veteran drink historians to take up the shovel and continue excavating.

On this trip, we found the twelfth- and thirteenth-century connections between English scholars and the early Arab alchemists that inspired research and experimentation with potable dis-tillates. We learned how thirteenth-century Franciscan friar Roger Bacon forwarded these inquiries in his search for a super-medicine, triggering the curiosity of fellow English, Irish, and Scot monastic alchemists by the late fifteenth century.

We now know that in fifteenth-century Germany, the distilling arts were a domestic pursuit just like brewing and that housewives distilled a juniper berry spirit, using affordable beer instead of wine to concoct their 'water of juniper berries'. Thanks to Johannes Gutenberg's printing press, distillation knowledge became available to women and the broader public, not just men in friars' frocks. And thanks to printed books this information was translated into other languages. German surgeon Hieronymous Brunschwig penned the first printed distillation book to get translated into English and published in London in 1527. So even though we know that distillation was around long enough for it to be referenced in the fourteenth century in Chaucer's *Canterbury Tales*, we know that in the next century, English monks, housewives, alchemists, and apothecaries busied themselves on a variety of different stills.

English royalty's involvement in introducing spirits consumption to the court and to the gentry began as early as Henry VIII and Elizabeth I. The rising number of recipes readers could make thanks to printed advice manuals suggests the rapid progression that transpired in spirit drinking's popularity.

Paired with the rise of conspicuous consumption and the retailing of spirits as not just medicines but as pleasurable potables, social drinking became a trend that really took off when James I's wife Queen Anne of Denmark imported the Danish royal court's habit of sipping spirits. The royal couple's physicians then contributed to the professionalisation of the distilling trade: standardising recipes such as *aqua fructum*, which is the earliest recorded recipe to approximate what we now consider to be modern-day gin.

While Londoners were enjoying the new potable, the royal household was sinking deeper and deeper into debt. (Those bejewelled gowns for both sexes and outrageous banquets cost more than the Treasury had to pay the mounting bills.)

The solution—the excise scheme—exploited the English habit for enjoying a pint and the tipple or two, taxing the brewers and distillers for their wares. Although some historians claimed that this tax system led to the decline of the English brewing trade, we've shown that was not the case. The shift to spirits consumption was based on the fad and fashion of keeping up with the Joneses. Nothing more and nothing less.

But what Londoners were drinking depended greatly on whether they were buying the rectified, sweetened spirits of the licenced distillers who were members of the Worshipful Company of Distillers or the compounded spirits produced by unlicenced distillers, who did not always subscribe to the most healthful adulterations. But how else was a poor person going to emulate the drinking culture of his or her uppers? It's the truth of the so-called Gin Craze: What the rich were drinking wasn't the same stuff the poor were swilling. But that leads to the fact that, in truth, there never really was a Gin Craze. It was the product of temperance and tabloid propaganda of the highest order. And the so-called eight 'gin acts' were not directed solely at gin production. These parliamentary statutes were aimed to regulate the distillation of everything from brandy to 'sweets' to geneva to gin to anything else that could be extracted from a still—not just gin.

For the same reason beer fell out of favour amongst London's sippers when spirits came on the scene, spirits fell out of favour with the invention and rising popularity of stout and porter beers. That is, until technological advancements such as the invention of the hydrometer to measure alcohol strength and the continuous column still which made it possible to make large quantities of considerably purer spirit. With this industrialisation of the distilling trade and a shift in consumer tastes to less sweet spirits, Plain Gin, London Gin, and eventually London Dry Gin came to the fore.

But as nineteenth distiller Charles Tovey noted the 'taste in the flavour of Gin varies in different localities, and that which may not be palatable in one county may be distilled in another.'

Such is the character of the world's most beloved cocktail spirit. Born from a simple rectification of spirit extracted from beer and juniper berries, gin gradually evolved into a sweetened juniper distil-late enhanced with botanicals such as coriander and liquorice. With technological advancements in still design and alcohol measurement as well as changing tastes, larger quantities of this 'improved' spirit revitalised interest once again into whatb we call gin.

What transpired next with the birth of the Cocktail Age during the mid- to late-nineteenth century grain which elevated gin to its pinnacle of popularity is only part of the story. That highest of heights was followed by grain rationing between the First and Second World Wars that led to its lowest of lows, shifting consumer tastes away from this noble water for a few decades. But that, dear reader, is a story for another day.

BIBLIOGRAPHY

Acts of Parliament:
1 William & Mary, c.24.
1 William & Mary, c.34
10 George II, c. 17.
11 George II, c. 26.
11 George IV & William IV, c.62.
11 George IV and William IV, c. 51.
16 George II, c. 8.
2 George II, c. 17.
2 George II, c.5.
2 William & Mary, c.9.
2 William & Mary, c.9(19).
20 George II, c. 39.
21 James I, c.3.
24 George II, c. 40.
27 George III, c.31.
34 & 35 Henry VIII, c.8, 9.
4 George III, c.7.
4 George IV, c. 51.
52 George III c.87.
6 George II, c. 17.
6 George IV c. 80.
9 George II, c. 23.

Bodleian Library:
MS Ashmole 1441.

British Library:
'Sloane MS 345', http://www.bl.uk/manuscripts/
        [accessed 17 June 2016].
Lansdowne MS 1215, folio 7.

Custom House MS:
'Excise Revenue Accounts, 1662-1827'.

Parliamentary Archives:
HL/PO/JO/10/1/431/375.
HL/PO/JO/10/1/431/375(a).

RCB Library
D11/12, *Red Book of Ossory*.

The National Archives:
T64/172.

Printed Primary Sources:
A Society in Edinburgh, 'LXXVIII. An Account of the most remarkable Improvement and Discoveries in Physick made or proposed since the Beginning of the Year 1735', Medi-cal Essays and Observations, Vol. V (Edinburgh: Hamilton, Balfour, and Neill, 1752).

Al-Kindi, Ya'qub ibn Ishaq, *Kitab al-Taraffuq fial-ʾitr*, MS Topkapi Sarai, Istanbul, No. 62-1992.

Andrewe, Laurens, *The vertuose boke of distyllacyon of the water of all maner of herbes* (London: Laurens Andrewe, 1527).

Anonymous, *An English Herbal, or, A discovery of the physical vertues of all herbs in this Kingdom* (London: A. Cloners, 1690).

Anonymous, 'Christmas Miscellany', *The Era Sunday*, 30 December 1838.

Boorde, Andrew, *The Fryst Boke of the Introduction of Knowledge Made by Andrew Boorde of Physyche Doctor*, ed. by F.J. Furnivall (London: N. Trübner & Com 1870).

Boyle, Patrick, *The publican and spirit dealers' Daily Companion. Sixth edition* (London: Pat-rick Boyle, 1800).

Brunschiwg, Hieronymous, *Libre de arte distillandi* (Strasbourg: Johann Grüninger, 1500).

Bullock, Christopher, *The Cobbler of Preston, fifth edition* (London: S. Bladon, 1767).

Camden, William, THE HISTORIE OF THAT EVER *Most blessed and Glorious Em-presse, Queene ELIZA-BETH of happy renowne and matchlesse Fame* (London: Robert Vaughan, 1625).

Chaucer, Geoffrey, '8.2 The Canon's Yeoman's Prologue', lines 580-581, https://chaucer.fas.harvard.edu/pages/canons-yeomans-prologue-and-tale [accessed 10 January 2023].

Company of Distillers of London, *The Distiller of London*, ed. by Anistatia R. Miller and Jared M. Brown (London: Mixellany Limited, 2020).

——, *The Distiller of London*, ed. Thomas de Mayerne and Thomas Cademan (London: R. Bishop, 1639).

Cooper, Ambrose, *The Complete Distiller* (London: P. Vaillant, 1757).

D'Ewes, Sir Simonds and Bowes, Paul, 'The Journal of the House of Commons', *The Journals of all the Parliaments During the Reign of Queen Elizabeth: Both of the House of Lords and the House of Commons* (London: John Starkey, 1682).

de Mandeville, Bernard, *The Fable of Bees: Or, Private Vices, Publick Benefits* (London: J. Roberts, 1714).

Defoe, Daniel, *A Brief Case of the Distillers, and of the Distilling Trade in England, shewing how far it is the interest of England to encourage the said trade, as it is so considerable an advantage to the landed* interest, to the trade and navigation, to the public revenue, and to the employment of the poor. Humbly recommended to the Lords and Commons of Great Britain, in the present Parliament assembled. (London: Thomas Warner, 1725).

——The Novels and Miscellaneous Works of Daniel De Foe (London: D.A. Tall-boys, 1840).

Dickens, Charles, Sketches by Boz (London: Chapman, 1895).

Evelyn, John, The Diary of John Evelyn, Vol. I, ed. by William Bray (London: M Walter Bunne, 1901).

Falimirz, Stefan, O ziolach y o moczy gich (Krakow: Floria Ungler, 1534).

French, Dr. John, The art of distillation, or, A treatise of the choicest spagyrical preparations, experiments, and curiosities, performed by way of distillation: together with the description of the choicest furnaces and vessels used by ancient and modern chymists, and the anatomy of gold and silver ... in six books / by John French ...; to which is added in this fourth impression Sublimation and calcination in two books; as also The London-distiller (London: E. Cotes for T.Williams, 1667).

Gessner, Conrad and Morwen, Peter, A New Booke of Destillatyon of Waters, Called the Treasure of Euonymus (London: John Day, 1565).

Great Britain, 'A Petition to the Parliament of 1421 for Protective Legislation', Rotuli Parliamentorum, Vol. 4, ed. by J. Strachey, et al. (London: HMSO, 1767-77).

——, 'Accounts and Papers of the House of Commons: Miscellaneous session 23 January to 11 July 1821'.

——, 'House of Commons Journal Volume I 27 February 1621,' Journal of the House of Commons, Volume I, 1547-1629 (London, 1802).

——, *A Grant of certain Impositions upon Beer, Ale, and other Liquors, for the In-crease of his Majesty's Revenue during his Life, 1660* (12 Charles II, c.23) (London: HMSO).

——, *An Ordinance for Continuing the Excise*, 17 March 1654 (London: HMSO).

——, *An Ordinance for the speedy Raising and Leavying of Moneys by way of Charge and New-Impost, upon the severall Commodities, in a Schedule hereunto annexed con-tained, as well for the better secur-ing of Trade, as for the maintenance of the Forces raised for the defence of the King, Parliament, and Kingdom, both by Sea and Land, as for and towards the payment of the Debts of the Common-wealth, for which the Publike Faith is, or shall be ingaged*, 8 September 1643 (London: HMSO).

——, *An Ordinance for the speedy Rising and Leavying of Moneys, set by way of Charge or new Impost, on the severall Commodities mentioned in the Schedule hereun-to annexed*, 22 July 1643 (London: HMSO).

——, *Calendar of State Papers, Domestic Series of the reign of Charles I. 1633-1634, Volume 6* (London: HMSO, 1863).

——, *Titles of Patents of Invention Chronologically arranged From March 2, 1617 (14 Janes I.) to Octo-ber 1, 1852 (16 Victoriæ): Part I, Nos. 1 to 4,800, pages 1 to 784*, ed. by Bennett Woodcroft (Lon-don: HMSO, 1854).

Harris, Walter, *A description of the king's royal palace and gardens at Loo, together with a short account of Holland* (London: R. Roberts, 1699).

Harrison, William, *The Description of England: The Clas-sic Contemporary Account of Tudor Social Life*, ed. by Georges Edelen (New York: Dover Publica-tions, Inc., 1994), 228-229.

Hermanni, Philippus, *Een Constelijck Distileerboec* (Antwerp: Philip de Lens, 1552), 56.

House of Commons, 'A Return of the Distillers Names in England, Residences, and Counties situated in...', 26 June 1821.

——, 'ACCOUNTS relating to British Spirits, Raw and Rectified, in each Ex-cise Collection in England, in the Stocks of Rectifiers, 1821-1823', 21 June 1824.

——, 'An Account of the Quantity of Corn Wash: Distilled and by whom, be-tween 5th July 1789 and the 5th July 1820; distinguishing the Quantities distilled each Year,' 28 March 1821 (London: HMSO, 1822).

——, 'Copy of a LETTER to The Right Honourable the Chancellor of the Ex-chequer, from the Corn Distillers in England, respecting the conversion of Rum into Gin by the Rectifiers; dated 30th May 1825'.

——, 'RETURN' of Licensed Distillers in England, Scotland, and Ireland; specifying the Situation and Excise Collection in which such Distilleries are situate;...', 6 June 1851.

Lewis, William, *The New Dispensatory* (London: J. Nourse, 1753).

Markham, Gervase, *Countrey Contentment, or The English Huswife* (London: R. Jackson, 1615).

——, *Countrey contentments, in two bookes: the first, containing the whole art of riding great horses ... with the breeding, breaking, dyeting and ordring of them ... The second intituled The English housewife: containing the inward and outward vertues which ought to be in a compleate women: as her phisicke, cookery ... distillation, perfumes, ... brewing, baking, and all other things belonging to an household* (London: R. Jackson, 1615).

Montagu, Walter, *The Queen's Closet Opened* (London: E Blagrave, 1696).

Moryson, Fynes, *Itinerary; Book III, Glasgow edition, volume IV* (Glasgow: James MacLehose and Sons, 1908).

Muspratt, James Sheridan, *Chemistry: Theoretical, Practical & Analytical as Applied to The Arts and Manufactures*, Vol. I (London, William Mackenzie, 1860).

Neumann, Caspar, *The Chemical Works of Caspar Neumann, M.D. Abridged and Methodized with Large Addition, Second Edition, Volume II* (London: J. and F. Rivington, 1773).

Pedemontanus, Alexius Ruscello, *De' secreti del reuerendo donno Alessio Piemontese, prima parte, diuisa in sei libri* (Venice: Sigismondo Bordogna, 1555).

Plat, Hugh, *Delightes for Ladies, to Adorne Their Persons, Tables, Closets, and Distillatories* (London: Peter Short, 1602).

Prynne, William, *Histrio-mastrix: The Player's Scourage or Actor's Tragedy* (London: Print-ed by E.A. and W.I. for M. Sparke, 1633).

Puff von Shrick, *Michael, Von allen geprenten wassern* (Augsburg: n.p. 1481).

R.W.W., 'Selections from Different Authors, &c.', *The Cottager's Monthly Visitor for M.DCC.XXI, Vol. I* (London: F.C. & J. Rivington, 1821).

Royal College of Physicians of London, *The new dispensatory of the Royal College College of Physicians in London. With copious and accurate indexes. Faithfully translated from the Latin of the Pharmacopoia Londinensis, publish'd by order of the King and Council* (London: printed for the translator, and sold by W. Owen), 1746.

———, *Pharmacopoea Londinensis* (London: Edward Griffin, 1618).

Scotland, 'Exchequer Roll (Edinburgh, 1494), Accounts of Ballivi ad Extra, Stirling, 18 June 1494 to 12 August 1495,' *Accounts of the Lord High Treasurer of Scotland, vol. 1* (Edinburgh 1877).

Shaw, Peter, *Three Essays in Artificial Philosophy or Universal Chemistry* (London: J. Osborn and T. Longman, 1731).

Smith, George, *A Compleat Body of Distilling, Explaining the Mysteries of that Science in a most easy and familiar Manner* (London: Henry Lintot, 1738).

Strype, John, 'GLOVERS, TINNERS, DISTILLERS,' *The Survey of the Cities of London and Westminster, Book 5* (London: 1598, reprinted J.M. Dent & Sons, Ltd., 1720).

Tovey, Charles, *British & Foreign Spirits: Their History, Manufacture, Properties, etc.* (London: Whittaker & Co., 1864).

Ya'qub ibn Ishaq Al-Kindi, *Kitab al-Taraffuq fial-ʿitr*, MS Topkapi Sarai, Istanbul, No. 62-1992.

Y-Worth, William, *The compleat Distiller ... to which is added Pharmacopoeia Spagyrica no-va ... being a philosophical Sal-Armoniack ... etc. ... The second edition, with altera-tions ... Illustrated with copper sculptures* (London: J. Taylor, 1705).

Secondary Sources

Accum, Frederick, *A Treatise of Adulterations of Food and Culinary Poisons* (London: Longman, Rees, Hurst, Orme, and Brown, 1820).

Adamson, Robert, 'Roger Bacon', *Encyclopaedia Britannica, Ninth Edition, Vol 3* (Chicago: Encyclopaedia Britannica, 1911).

Allen, Katherine J., 'Manuscript Recipe Collections and Elite Domestic Medicine in Eighteenth-Century England' (unpublished thesis, University of Oxford, 2015).

Alowais, Aisha and Idriz, Mesut, 'Adelard of Bath', *Al-Adab Journal*, 1/139 (2021).

Anon., 'Distillation', *Industrial Engineering Chemistry*, 28/6 (1936).

Ashworth, William J., *Customs and Excise: Trade, Production, and Consumption in England, 1640-1845* (Oxford: Oxford University Press, 2003).

Bakkum, Barclay, 'A historical lesson from Franciscus Sylvius and Jacobus Sylvius', *Journal of Chiropractic Humanities*, 18(1) (2011).

Bayley, Stephen, *Gin* (Salisbury: Gin and Vodka Association of Great Britain, 1994).

Beier, Lucinda M., *Sufferers and Healers: The Experience of Illness in Seventeenth-Century England* (London: Routledge and Kegan Paul, 1987).

Berlin, Michael, *The Worshipful Company of Distillers: A Short History* (Chichester: Phillimore & Co. Ltd., 1996).

British Library, 'Shakespeare in print: 1. London book trade', https://www.bl.uk/treasures/ [accessed 6 February 2022].

Britten, James and Holland, Robert, *The dictionary of English plant-names, Part I* (London: Trübner & Co, 1886).

Bruning, Ted, *London Dry: The Real History of Gin* (Hayward, CA: White Mule Press, 2020).

Brüning, Volker Fritz, *Bibliographica Alchemica* (Munich: K G Saur Verlag GmbH, 2004).

Burke, Peter, 'Res et verba: conspicuous consumption in the early modern world,' *Consumption and*

the World of Goods, ed. by John Brewer and Roy
    Porter (London: Routledge, 1993).

Burnett, John, *Liquid Pleasures: A Social History of Drink
    in Modern Britain* (London: Routledge, 1999).

Chartres, John, 'No English Calvados? English distill-
    ers and the cider industry in the seventeenth
    and eighteenth centuries?', *English rural society
    1500-1800: Essays in honour of Joan Thirsk*, ed.
    by John Chartres and David Hey (Cambridge:
    Cambridge University Press, 1990).

Clark, Peter, 'The "Mother Gin" Controversy in the
    Early Eighteenth Century', *Transactions of the
    Royal Historical Society*, 38 (1988).

——, *The English Alehouse: A Social History 1200-1830*
    (Burnt Mill: Longman Group, 1983).

Cockaigne, Oswald, *Leechdomes, Wortcunning, and
    Starcraft of Early England* (London: Longman,
    Green, Longman, Roberts, and Green, 1864).

Costache, Iulia, 'The first Jewish settlements in the
    United Kingdom', Museum of Oxford <https://
    museumofoxford.org/ > [accessed 15 Decem-
    ber 2023].

Cressy, David, 'Levels of Illiteracy in England 1530-
    1730', *The Historical Journal*, 20/1 (1977).

Crow, M.B., 'Peter of Ireland: Teacher of St Thomas
    Aquinas', *Studies: An Irish Quarterly Review*,
    45/180 (1956).

Dietz, Frederick Charles, E*nglish Public Finance 1558-
    1641* (London: The Century Co., 1932).

Drummond, J.C. and Wilbreham, Anne, T*he English-
    man's Food: Five Centuries of English Diet* (Lon-
    don: Jonathan Cape, 1939, revised 1957).

Eisenstein, Elizabeth L., *The Printing Revolution in Early
    Modern Europe* (Cambridge: Cam-bridge Uni-
    versity Press, 1983).

Filby, Frederic Arthur, *A History of Food Adulteration and Analysis* (London: G. Allen & Unwin Limited, 1934).

Flavin, Susan, Meltonville, Marc, Taverner, Charlie, Reid, Joshua, Lawrence, Stephen, Belloch-Mollina, Carlos, and Morrissey, John, 'Understanding Early Modern Beer: An Interdisciplinary Case-Study', *The Historical Journal*, 66 (2023).

Fleming, Peter, *Time, Space and Power in Late Medieval Bristol* (unpublished working paper, University of West England, 2013).

Forbes, R. J., *Short History of the Art of Distillation: From the Beginnings up to the Death of Cellier Blumenthal* (Leiden: Brill, 1948).

French, Richard Valpy, *Nineteen Centuries of Drink England: A History* (London: National Temperance Publication Depot, 1884).

G.B. (n.d.), 'On the Early Use of Aqua Vitæ in Ireland', *Ulster Journal of Archaeology*, 6 (1858).

Garbers, Karl, *Kitab kimiya' al-'itr wat-tas idat : Buch über die Chemie des Parfüms und die Destillationen; ein Beitrag zur Geschichte der arabischen Parfümchemie und Drogenkunde aus dem 9* (Leipzig: Brockhaus, 1948).

Getz, Faye, 'Roger Bacon and Medicine: the paradox of the Forbidden Fruit and the Secrets of Long Life,' *Roger Bacon and the Sciences: Commemorative Essays*, ed. by Jeremiah Hackett (New York: Brill, 1997).

Gin Guild, 'The 1495 Gin', https://www.theginguild.com/ginopedia/ [accessed 18 December 2020].

Griffenhagen, George B. and Harvey, James, 'Old English Patent Medicines in America', *Contribu-*

tions from the Museum of History and Technology, Paper 10 (1959).

Halleux, Robert, 'The Reception of Arabic Alchemy in the West', *Encyclopedia of the History of Arabic Science. Vol. 3*, ed. by Roshdi Rashed (London: Routledge, 1996).

Hayward, Trish and Hayward, Peter, 'Pewter Stills', *Journal of the Pewter Society*, Autumn 2013.

Hoskins, W.G., 'Harvest Fluctuations and English Economic History, 1620-1759', *The Agricultural History Review*, 16/1 (1968).

Howard, Vicki and Stobart, Jon, 'Arcades, shopping centres, and shopping malls', *The Routledge Companion to the History of Retailing*, ed. by Jon Stobart and Vicki Howard (London: Routledge, 2018).

Hubbard, Eleanor, 'Reading, Writing, and Initiating Female Literacy in Early Modern London', *Journal of British Studies*, 54/3 (2015).

Jones, W.R. 'Franciscan Education and Monastic Libraries: Some Documents', *Traditio*, 30 (1974).

Kibre, Pearl, 'Alchemical Writings Ascribed to Albertus Magnus,' *Speculum*, 17/4 (Oct 1942).

Kirton, John William, *Intoxicating Drinks: Their History & Mystery* (London: Ward, Lock & Co., 1879).

Kleineke,, Hannes 'The medicines of Katherine, Duchess of Norfolk 1463-1471', Medical His-tory, 59/4 (2015), 520.

Kockmann, Norbert, '200 Years in Innovation in Distillation', ChemBioEng Reviews 1/1 (2014), 41

Koopmans, Joop W. , *Historical Dictionary of the Netherlands* (Lanham, MD: Rowman & Lit-tlefield Publishers, 2015).

Lawlor, Hugh Jackson, 'Calendar of the Liber Ruber of the Diocese of Ossory', *Proceedings of the Royal Irish Academy: Archaeology, Culture, History, Literature*, 27 (1908).

Lehmann-Haupt, Hellmut E., 'Johannes Gutenberg'. *Encyclopedia Britannica*, 18 May. 2023, https://www.britannica.com/biography/Johannes-Gutenberg [accessed 16 August 2023].

LeMay, Richard, 'Roger Bacon's Attitude toward the Latin Translations and Translators of the Twelfth and Thirteenth Centuries,' *Roger Bacon and the Sciences: Commemorative Essays*, ed. Jeremiah Hackett (New York: Brill, 1997).

Lucas Bols Distillery, '5 questions about Genever with Piet van Leijenhorst', https://bols.com/bartendingacademy [accessed 12 February 2022].

——, 'Lucas Bols Distillery', https://www.diffordsguide.com/ [accessed 12 February 2022].

——, 'What a Distillery!', http://www.lucasbols.com/history.asp [accessed 12 February 2022].

Miller, Anistatia, '"A most noble water of vertues": revisiting English gin's origins and its relationship with beer', *Brewing History,* 195 (2023)

Miller, Anistatia and Brown, Jared, 'Pimm's Cup', *The Oxford Companion to Spirits & Cocktails* (Oxford: Oxford University Press, 2022).

——, *Spirituous Journey: A History of Drink, Volume One* (London: Mixellany Limited, 2009).

Minkowski, William L., 'Women Healers of the Middle Ages: Selected Aspects of Their History', *American Journal of Public Health*, 82/2 (1992).

Moran, Bruce T, *Distilling Knowledge: Alchemy, Chemistry, and the Scientific Revolution* (London: Harvard University Press, 2005).

Needleman, Herbert L., 'History of Lead Poisoning in the World', Center for Biological Diver-sity < https://www.biologicaldiversity.org/campaigns/get_the_lead_out/pdfs/health/Needleman_1999.pdf> [accessed 21 February 2024].

Nicholls, James, 'Drinking Cultures and Consumption in England: Historical Trends and Policy Implications', *Memorandum AL 59* (2009) https://publications.parliament.uk/ [accessed 15 June 2022].

Old Bailey Proceedings Online, December 1722. Trial of Barthia Fisher (t17221205-3). https://www.oldbaileyonline.org/ [accessed: 18 December 2023].

———, Trial of Thomas Bonnamy (t17321206-68) https://www.oldbaileyonline.org/ [accessed: 18 December 2023].

Old Bailey Proceedings Online, January 1726. Trial of Mary Jolly (t17260114-46). https://www.oldbaileyonline.org/ [accessed: 18 December 2023].

Old Bailey Proceedings Online. https://www.oldbaileyonline.org/ [accessed: 18 December 2023].

Oxford English Dictionary, 'gin, n.1a'.

———, 'whisky', n.1.

———, gorst, n.

Parent, André, 'Franciscus Sylvius on Clinical Teaching, Iatrochemistry and Brain Anatomy', *The Canadian Journal of Neurological Sciences*, 43 (2016).

Pelling, Margaret and Webster, Charles, 'Medical Practitioners', *Health, Medicine and Mortal-ity in the Sixteenth Century*, ed. Charles Webster (Cambridge: Cambridge University Press, 1979).

Porter, Roy, 'Consumption: disease of the consumer society', *Consumption and the World of Goods*, ed. by John Brewer and Roy Porter (London: Routledge, 1993).

Price, P. Vandyke, *The Penguin Book of Spirits and Liqueurs* (Harmondsworth, 1980).

Reay, Barry, *Microhistories: Demography, Soceity, and Culture in Rural England, 1800-1930* (Cambridge: Cambridge University Press, rev. ed. 2002).

Roueché, Berton, *The Neutral Spirit: A Portrait of Alcohol* (Boston: Little Brown and Company, 1960).

Shaw, Peter, *Three Essays in Artificial Philosophy or Universal Chemistry* (London: J. Osborn and T. Longman, 1731).

Simon, Andre, 'The Art of Distillation', lecture delivered at The Vintner's Hall by the Wine Trade Club, 1912.

Slack, Paul, 'Mirrors of Health and Treasures of Poor Men: The Uses of the Vernacular Medical Literature of Tudor England,' *Health, Medicine and Mortality in the Sixteen Century*, ed. by Charles Webster (Cambridge: Cambridge University Press, 1979).

Stationers Company, 'Tradition and Heritage', https://www.stationers.org/ [accessed 6 February 2022].

Stobart, Anne, 'The Making of Domestic Medicine: Gender, Self-Help and Therapeutic Determination in Household Healthcare in South-West England in the Late Seventeenth Century' (unpublished thesis, Middlesex University, 2008).

Stobart, Jon, 'A history of shopping: the missing link between retail and consumer revolutions',

Journal of Historical Research in Marketing, 2/3 (2010).

Stopes, Henry, *Malt and Malting: An Historical and scientific and Practical Treatise, Showing as Clearly as Existing Knowledge Permits What Malt Is and How to Make It* (London: Lyon, 1885).

Styles, John, 'Manufacturing, consumption and design in eighteenth-century England', *Consumption and the World of Goods*, ed. by John Brewer and Roy Porter (London: Routledge, 1993).

Survey of London, 'Whitechapel Sports Centre, Durward Street' < https://surveyoflondon.org/map/feature/615/detail/> [accessed 21 January 2024].

Sweet, H., 'Glossary (MS Cambridge, Corpus Christi College 144)', *The Oldest English Texts* (London: Published for the Early English Text Society by N. Trübner).

Thirsk, Joan, *Economic Policy and Projects: The Development of a Consumer Society in Early Modern England* (Oxford: Clarendon Press, 1978; reprinted 1988).

Thomson, Glady Scott, *Life in a Noble Household, 1641-1700,* Bedford Historical Series, I, (London: Jonathan Cape, 1940).

Tlusty, B. Ann ,'Water of Life, Water of Death: The Controversy over Brandy and Gin in Early Modern Augsburg,' *Central European History,* 31/1 (1998).

Toomer, G.J., 'The Medieval Background', *Eastern Wisdom and Learning: The Study of Arabic in Seventeenth-century England* (Oxford: Oxford University Press, 1996).

Trevor-Roper, Hugh Redwald, *Europe's physician: the various life of Sir Theodore de Mayerne* (London: Yale University Press, 2006).

Trotter, Thomas, *An Essay, Medical, Philosophical, and Chemical on Drunkenness and its Effects on the Human Body* (London: Printed for T.N. Longman, and O. Rees, 1804).

Unger, Richard W., *Beer in the Middle Ages and the Renaissance* (Philadelphia: University of Pennsylvania Press, 2004).

Unwin, George, *The Gilds and Companies of London, Fourth ed.* (London: Frank Case & Company, 1963).

Unwin, Tim, *Wine and Vine: An Historical Geography of Viticulture and the Wine Trade* (London: Routledge: 1991).

Van Schoonenberghe, Eric, 'Genever (gin): A Spirit Drink full of History, Science and Technology', *Sartonia*, 12 (1999), 99.

——, *Jenever in de Lage Landen* (Brugge: Stuchting Kunstboek, 1996).

Various, *Medische En Technische Middelnederlandse Recepten*, ed. Willy L. Braekman (Ghent: Koninklijke Vlaamse Academie, 1975).

Voigts, Linda Ehrsam, 'The Master of the King's Stillatories', *The Lancastrian Court, Harlaxton Medieval Studies* 13 (Donington: Shaun Tyas, 2003).

Warner, Jessica, 'The Naturalization of Beer and Gin in Early Modern England', *Contemporary Drug Problems*, 24/2 (1997).

——, *Craze: Gin and Debauchery in an Age of Reason* (London: Profile Book, 2004).

Watney, John, *Mother's Ruin: A History of Gin* (London: Peter Owen, 1976).

Watt, Diane, 'Mary the Physician: Women, Religion and Medicine in the Middle Ages', *Medicine, Religion and Gender in Medieval Culture*, ed. by N. Yoshikawa (Martlesham, Suffolk: Boydell & Brewer, 2015).

Webster, Thomas, and William, Mrs., *An Encyclopæ-dia of Domestic Economy* (New York: Harper & Brothers, 1815).

Wellcome Collection, explanation in Von den ausger-branntan wassern https://wellcomecollec-tion.org/works/pakjtgzm/images [accessed 16 November 2023].

Williams, Steven J., 'Roger Bacon and the Secret of Secrets', *Roger Bacon and the Sciences: Com-memorative Essays*, ed. Jeremiah Hackett (New York: Brill, 1997).

Wilson, Constance Anne, *Water of Life: A History of Wine-Distilling and Spirits 500 BC to AD 2000* (Totnes, Devon: Prospect Books, 2006).

World Data Bank, 'Physicians (per 1,000 people) - United Kingdom' <https://data.worldbank.org/indicator/> [accessed 21 February 2024].

Worshipful Society of Apothecaries, 'Origins', https://www.apothecaries.org/history/ [accessed 3 May 2020].

Wrigley, Anthony, 'Urban Growth and Agricultural Change: England and the Continent in the Early Modern Period,' *The Journal of Interdis-ciplinary History*, 15/4 (Spring 1985).

SUBJECT Index

234

Appendix

S HALL WE BUST one last myth? The gin and tonic was not invented in India as an anti-malarial. British troops did not drink it as part of their rations. And, honestly, no one in the history of tonic water ever drank is as an anti-malarial. That was made up by a sloppy writer sometime around the 1970s, and has been echoed ever since.

The cinchona tree is native to South America. According to a 1712 German book, *Dissertatio Solennis Medica de Quinquina Europaeorum*, the first Europeans to encounter cinchona—and more importantly to encounter natives using it to treat malarial symptoms such as fever and nausea—were Spanish jesuit priests in occupied Peru. This claim is further detailed in an 1817 French paper, *Zuma or La Découverte du Quinquina*. The Spanish began importing cinchona bark to Europe, and soon its use was widespread, primarily for treating fevers and dyspepsia.

In 1820, French scientists Joseph Pelletier and Joseph Caventou successfully isolated and extracted a sulphate of quinine (which they also named), using

QUININE WINE.—The TONIC or QUININE WINE contains, diffused through an agreeable menstruum, and combined with auxiliary aromatics, the newly-discovered alkaline principle of the Peruvian Bark, which has been administered with extraordinary success by the most eminent Physicians in Europe. It possesses decided superiority over all other preparations of Bark or stomachic bitters in remedying indigestion, promoting appetite, and restoring the action of the stomach, in cases of habitual or occasional derangement. It will be found of unequalled efficacy in the cure of Intermittent Fevers, and highly serviceable in all Gouty, Scrofulous, and Debilitated Habits.—Sold by the sole Proprietor, J. BASS, Chemist, No. 76, New Bond-street, London, in bottles, 4s. 6d., 11s., and 1l. 1s. each; also by Mr. C. R. Weller, Chemist, 63, Threadneedle-street.

alcohol and sulphuric acid. By 1824, quinine lozenges were available—with no mention of treating malaria. Tonic or quinine wine emerged the same year, and though treating fevers was mentioned at the end of the ad, malaria wasn't mentioned.

It has been claimed that the Dutch mixed genever and tonic by 1825. This is likely a misunderstanding from published references to Schiedam Schnapps tonic, which was simply a 'tonic' or health-restoring liquid in the pre-tonic water sense of the word.

Over the next three decades, quinine continued to be prescribed by doctors and sold directly to the European public primarily to treat digestive ailments for the simple reason that the majority of Europeans were unlikely to encounter a malaria-bearing mosquito in the lifetimes, but were prone to near-constant food poisoning.

Meanwhile, in India, the majority of the British troops were actually recruited locally, and their preferred intoxicants included *bhang, charas, ganja,* opium, toddy, and arrack.[1] Thus, they were an unlikely group to suddenly mix gin, lime sugar, sparkling water and quinine.

The earliest known ad for tonic water appeared on 24 July 1858, promoting Pitt's Aerated Quinine Tonic Water, and predicting that this would replace the brandy and soda doctors recommended as a daily drink. Prior to this ad, even months prior, tonic water meant nothing more than health-giving liquid. There were ads for tonic waters for the hair, a land ad touting a stream of tic water flowing through the property, etc. It was only after Pitt's and other quinine tonic waters emerged that the term took on its modern meaning. But for Pitt's, sales foundered in London and within four years, Pitt's was pursuing sales far from England in the British colonies. Ads appeared in newspapers in Singapore, New Zealand, Australia and India.

Around 1873, stories appeared in London newspapers of people arriving from India and seeking to quench their thirst with gin and tonics. And thus, the gin and tonic was born.

---

1.   Christopher Cavin, 'Intoxicants and the Indian Colonial Army: Consumption and Control, 1857-1919' (unpublished thesis, University of Strathclyde, 2018).

ABOUT THE AUTHORS

J ARED BROWN, MA, co-founder and master distiller of Sipsmith Limited, is a multi-award winning drink historian whom with his wife Anistatia Miller have written a few dozen books including *Shaken Not Stirred: A Celebration of the Martini* and the two-volume *Spirituous Journey: A History of Drink* plus a few hundred articles about drinks, spirits, and how to make them.

Brown was co-recipient of the 2021 Helen David Lifetime Achievement Award and the 2010 IESC Communicator of the Year Award with his wife, drink historian Anistatia Miller, MA, MSc (Ox). She is the director of Mixellany Limited, a drinks consultancy and publishing company. After 35 years in the publishing industry overlapping 30 years of spreading the gospel of drink with Brown, Miller is finishing her PhD in History from the University of Bristol on the history of early-modern brewing in fifteenth- through early eighteenth-century Bristol.

Milton Keynes UK
Ingram Content Group UK Ltd.
UKHW011339150624
444218UK00004B/206